# THE RESTLESS CHURCH

J. B. LIPPINCOTT COMPANY / PHILADELPHIA / NEW YORK

# THE RESTLESS CHURCH

A RESPONSE TO THE COMFORTABLE PEW

EDITED BY WILLIAM KILBOURN

Printed in the United States of America
Library of Congress Catalog Card No.: 66-18678

# PREFACE

Let one review of Pierre Berton's *The Comfortable Pew* speak for hundreds of others. The editor of *The Link*, "A Protestant Magazine for Armed Forces Personnel," reviewed Berton's book in the February, 1966 issue of his magazine. The column, ironically, is called "Books Are Friendly Things," but the review begins, "This is a shocking book written by a man who has left the church." It continues:

*And more amazing – the invitation to write it came from a church group. The main thesis of the book is that the church has failed. He gives the church no credit, no plus factors at all; it has failed – period. And his suggestions for rejuvenation are somewhat as follows: Become pacifists; quit preaching; lower moral standards, especially sex standards; get rid of God; do away with church buildings; get the church persecuted; and wait for a new Messiah. Someone needs to write a reply – someone within the church – who will be discerning but who will be fair. Mr. Berton would throw out the baby with the bath water.*

*The Restless Church* is that reply, written by a number of somebodies, most of them from within the Church.

One hundred years ago occasional village atheists would publish attacks on the churches, only to succeed in uniting the clergy against themselves. The preachers would devastate them with their joint defences of God and Church. Today, village atheists who care to publish are few. When Anglicans in Canada subsidized a nationally known agnostic to criticize, the preachers did not unite against him. This book is evidence of the varieties of response: some say the critic went too far and missed the point; to others, he seemed superficial and mild. The believer finds himself bewildered between comfortable pew and restless church – a maddening place to be, for those who care and are faithful.

*1* / Denis de Rougemont must have chosen his words with care when he said that "the situation in which a Christian finds himself today is utterly *insane* – that is, if he feels obligated to live and think according to his faith." De Rougemont described three contexts, and they have much to do with the contents of this book. It is "a world where that faith is denied, more or less serenely ignored, or, even worse, where Christianity is accepted and ridiculed under the forms of its traditional deviations, its caricatures: in short, in a world where it does not exist.'*

Who bothers, in the first place, to *deny* the faith in North America? Who, that is, is enraged enough to stand outside the churches and express his offence over against the offence of the gospel? Now and then a Walter Kaufmann will pay a compliment by attacking God and religion and the churches. "Only where God is radically proclaimed and believed can he be so radically denied" (Gerhard Ebeling). But few formal systematic assaults of denial are mounted. A reflective man of faith must sometimes wonder why. In this book, Pierre Berton's motives and abilities as denier receive extensive discussion.

According to de Rougemont, the faith can also be serenely *ignored*. A shrugged shoulder is perhaps the greatest insult to faith and church. In the hope that the shrug could be elevated to a system, the Anglicans stimulated their lapsed son Berton to stop ignoring and to start criticizing. His book revealed how much he remembered, how much he hoped, how much he regretted, and how much he wanted changed. He revealed himself to be a card-carrying member of what Paul Tillich called the "latent church" (as opposed to a visible, confessing communion). In the process, he proved how much he was still obsessed with quasi-religious concerns. He twitted people; he tweaked noses. He complained. He programed.

---

*The Christian Opportunity* (New York: Holt, Rinehart and Winston, 1963), p. 10.

To rescue one man from the circle of the serene ignorers is a significant but isolated achievement. The *affaire Berton*, however, is memorable because it stimulated wide controversy of a kind that is helpful both to pro-Church and anti-Church people. On de Rougemont's third level, it revealed just how much acceptance and ridicule had been devoted to "the forms of [Christianity's] traditional deviations, its *caricatures*." *The Restless Church* advances the debate by considering in what ways Berton dealt with deviation and caricature and in what ways he dealt with something integral to the faith and the Church.

About half the authors in this book celebrate Berton, rejoice in his passion, feel liberated by his concern. Others stimulate debate by stifling yawns and saying in effect, "Now stand aside and let the veteran critics from within the churches take over." William Stringfellow and Peter Berger, to name two, suggest that Berton's is a velvet-gloved treatment of a church which is hand in glove with culture. Writes Berger: "Pierre Berton concludes his book, holding out cultural success with one hand and crucifixion with the other. This is more than inconsistency. It is nonsense."

2 / The "comfortable pew" is a piece of furniture which symbolizes self-satisfied and unself-critical churches. (Why restrict it to Anglicanism or to Canada?) Such churches are productive of values which sanction and congratulate a smug or even a lethal society. They do not judge or save it. They come to the support of integrative religious values but reject disruptive prophetic concerns. They baptize the O.K. world, make no enemies, deny their own true vision, attempt no great things for God, and are politically dependent upon middle-class culture for support.

In some respects, Berton's criticisms on this score apply more to the churches of the mid-1950s than those of the mid-1960s. A decade ago, in the high-Eisenhower years when, as Ronald Steel puts it,* there was an "historical intermission when America stopped off for a snooze while the world churned inconsiderably on," the churches of the United States and of Canada (which needed no Eisenhower) breathed the spirit of the times. Church leaders worked frantically and frenetically to cajole Christians to join the snooze in comfortable pews.

---

*The New York Review of Books*, January 6, 1966, p. 17.

The revival bore the seeds of surfeit, and by the late 1950s fed-up critics (among them Stringfellow and Berger) published analyses of revival-type personal religion and social ideology. By 1960 some of us "critics and prophets" were counting our credit cards, deciding that the establishment's *danegeld* was buying us off, and that prophecy was hard to sustain in such a situation. There were better things to do: participate in some social questions, raise questions of truth in theology, make constructive suggestions for reform of the Church.

The popularity of Berton's book illustrates not only the fact that clerical or professional criticisms had become old stuff but that authentic words from "outsiders" could still have telling effect. Insiders had left the field too early. They thought they had made their point when they heard people talk about new structures of ministry, new breeds of clergymen, new theology, new morality, new laymen, renewed Church. They were more hard-pressed to discover signs that a basic reform had taken place, that the reaction and revolution of the 1960s had really jostled many out of the comfortable pew. Berton mopped up; the notoriety of his work was a sign of its necessity.

3 / The intervening years since the revival have revealed how little the churches have come up with in the matter of sex, race, peace, and other issues raised by Berton. The Viet Nam crisis in the United States revealed how many comfortable pew-sitters would rise to cheer militarism. The racial crisis was a happier story, for it evoked creative church leadership; but it exposed the extent of delay, resistance, or at least halfheartedness of many churchgoers in the matter.

During the 1960s we have become aware of tension between the new breed and the durable pew-sitters who foot the bills. Laymen (including the former editor of *Fortune* in that magazine in December, 1965) asked just what it was for which laymen were paying. Theologians chatted nonchalantly about the death of God. Anything to blow away now the incense which still cast a spell on those in the "comfortable pew"! To most authors in *The Restless Church*, Berton stands between revival and revolution, dealing with deviations and caricatures of the Church in both eras. It is not likely that Berton's critics will wholly succeed in tipping over comfortable pews, because some deviation and caricature seems to adhere to religious life in a complex society.

People in our modern, pluralist, secular world have been successfully devising a civic or societal religion much like the *Romanitas* of the ancient world or the Christendom of the Middle Ages. The new religion in and around the churches absorbs many Christian elements; most new religions tend to absorb as much as they displace. Modern nationalism and religious defences of industrial, affluent societies will tend, at least in North America, to contain rich reminiscences of Christianity. Versions of Christianity helped us over the hump toward political democracy and industrial productivity. It is not likely that we can throw off this faith and still keep the culture which had been bonded to it.

Some people call the comfortable new religion "secularization." Others, along with sociologist J. Milton Yinger, are content to speak of a radical religious *change* carried on under the continuity of old symbols ("pew," "Church," etc.). That some civic or societal religion is inevitable is a commonly accepted observation. Whether it is good or bad depends on what one thinks of the prophetic or Protestant or classical Christianity which is supposed to measure or judge society.

On this issue, too, the authors in this book are divided. Some people accept Bertonism because it symbolizes destruction of inbred and inverted churches so that Christians can be free for the secular world. Others ask whether the churches are not somehow necessary as living communities in which the word is heard, where language is formed, where norms for judging the world in order to save it are established. Peter Berger, always adept at bringing up embarrassing subjects, contends that the churchless, pro-world Christians, who are so ready with their embrace of what is, are engaging in theological self-liquidation: "Norman Vincent Peale, with whose moral positions the 'rascals' disagree so fiercely, differs not one iota from the basic ideological procedure that they employ themselves" in the embrace of the secular as it is.

People who agree and who tend to reject obsessive avant-gardism and glib attempts at relevance should welcome in this book Stringfellow's theological concern for baptism, Eugene Fairweather's defense of the Christian tradition, and Monica Furlong's almost hopeful love letter to the Church. They keep *The Restless Church* from ideological neatness. The editor could have made up a book of pro-Berton people inside the churches. He could as easily have gathered people who would reply in anti-Berton terms. Most contributors to the book as you find it here direct energies elsewhere: they are interested in separating the church from its caricatures and Berton from his.

4 / We would find few reasons to commend a book given over to petty argument: "I can be more radical than he, ha-ha! and I am *in* the Church!" or, "The u.s. and Canada are on different time-tables of secularization," or, "Berton belongs to the 1950s, not to the 1960s." Instead, *The Restless Church* relates to enduring and even fateful problems of believers who feel obligated to live and think according to their faith in an utterly insane situation – to refer to de Rougemont's text once more. Problems of the integrity of the Church and the understanding of the world are discussed here. The issues relate not merely to the turn from religious revival in one decade to revolution in another. They are part of a chapter in the long history of Christian witness in a secularizing world. They reveal steps and side steps which serious people make as they try to think about God and world after centuries of scientific and industrial change, of political revolution.

An effective denier Berton may not be; that he can no longer ignore the Church has become evident. That he and his respondents have quickened a debate about deviations and caricatures of the faith over against what they hope to see as The Real Thing promises to be their permanent contribution to those who would shun caricatures as they would shun idols.

MARTIN E. MARTY
*Chicago, Illinois*
*January, 1966*

*Martin E. Marty is associate editor of* The Christian Century *and associate professor of Church History at the University of Chicago. He is also the author of* The Infidel *and* Varieties of Unbelief.

# CONTENTS

# INTRODUCTION

In 1963 the Anglican Church's Department of Religious Education decided to ask an agnostic to take a critical look at the Church, and to write a book about what he saw. Pierre Berton, probably the best known journalist and television interviewer in Canada, was invited to help the Church in this way, not only because he was an outspoken critic of Canadian society and could be expected to speak to and for a great many people, but also because, as one Church spokesman put it, he was a man of integrity who could be relied upon to make a strong but fair case for whatever he decided to say. He had also been brought up in the Anglican Church, but left it in his twenties when he decided he no longer believed its teachings.

Anglicans in 1963 were beginning to speak a good deal about becoming "a listening Church" and engaging in a dialogue with the world, particularly during the Church's World Congress in Toronto that summer. But the actual invitation to an outsider – a real person – to start talking came as a surprise. News of the project let loose a storm of controversy in the press, and motions of protest were closely contested in several official Church bodies. On balance, however, the reaction to the idea was favourable, or at least open-minded, and the dominant mood appeared to be that expressed by the Primate, Archbishop Howard Clark, who commented drily on some of the extreme statements for and against the book (which was as yet not even researched, let alone drafted) that he would wait until it had been written and he had read it to see whether or not he approved.

When it was ready, in January of 1965, it provided another surprise. A book often reaches the Canadian best-seller list with a sale of less than 5,000 copies. A first printing of 5,000 is rare, and both the Church and the publisher thought they were taking a considerable risk when they originally decided to order 16,000. Within a few days, however, it was clear that *The Comfortable Pew* would break all existing records in the history of Canadian publishing. Not counting the British and American editions, there are to date 170,000 copies in print.

Quite apart from its sales record (which may or may not reflect a book's real significance), the publication of *The Comfortable Pew* has clearly been a remarkable event in Canadian life. It was the subject of hundreds of newspaper editorials, articles, and cartoons, and several dozen radio and television programs. One city newspaper published no less than eight different reviews of it. There can scarcely be a Protestant church or parish hall in the country in which the name of the book or its author was not at least mentioned in 1965, and in some, at times, it almost seemed as if people were talking of nothing else. One parish put on twenty-one noon hour talks during weekdays in Lent. A series of seven Sunday evening sermons about the book preached in a London United Church was not untypical. Several thousand church groups appear to have discussed it at meetings.

It became the theme of a Kinsmen's parade float in British Columbia, and at Bishop's University, Lennoxville, almost the whole class of two hundred students in the required religion course chose to write about *The Comfortable Pew* on their final exam. The title itself (or variations on it) contributed a new phrase to the Canadian language. The *Canadian Underwriter* speculated about the desirability of getting Pierre Berton to write a book on the insurance industry – to be called *The Uncomfortable Backlash*. The Board chairman of the *B.C. Professional Engineer* wrote an editorial called "The Comfortable Sliderule" and asked, "if the Protestant church can invite this sort of self-criticism, can the Engineering profession do less?"

As for opinions about its merit, the book was called everything from clear, fresh, and penetrating to trite, dated, and confused. The Moderator of the United Church of Canada said that it should be required reading in every theological seminary. Charlotte

Whitton, the broadcaster and former mayor of Ottawa, saw it as an attempt by "Anglican headquarters to disrupt and destroy the Faith as we know it." The rector of one city church called it "an ecclesiastical *Fanny Hill*, the product of a mediocre mind," while another invited its author to come to his church to preach. A British Columbia rural priest wrote to *The Canadian Churchman* to say that though he was originally opposed to the book being written, he now regarded it "as possibly the most important document since Martin Luther nailed up his ninety-five theses." Pierre Berton himself was described variously as "a brilliant young man deceived by Satan," and a "mediocre author approaching dotage." He was publicly compared to the prophet Amos, John the Baptist, Tom Paine, Big Brother of 1984, and Balaam's ass. "Thou art Pierre," one writer commented, "and upon this rock will I build my Church."

What is unusual, however, is that the book seems to have set off a genuine clash of ideas, a debate and dialogue at many levels, and a serious attempt by many people to study some of the issues it raises. And such a result is no mean achievement in a country where ideas are not normally taken seriously and are more apt to be praised, blasted, or ignored than carefully examined.

Part Six includes an open letter to the Church by Arnold Edinborough, well-known Anglican layman and editor of *Saturday Night*, written in September 1965, immediately after he had taken part in the Church's history-making General Synod in Vancouver. This is followed by an excerpt from an interview by Jack Rutherford of the Canadian Broadcasting Corporation with Professor Harvey Cox, whose stimulating book, *The Secular City*,[1] may well prove to be one of the most important theological works of our time.

First and foremost, however, this present book is intended as a response by people speaking from their experience of the Judaeo-Christian tradition, to a liberal humanist and his view of the Church. It is a discussion of questions raised by Pierre Berton, not a point by point reply to him. It is intended for anyone interested in the issues involved in the dialogue between Christianity and humanism, not for people who happen to have read *The Comfortable Pew* and want to see it refuted.

Part One covering five of the great social and moral issues of our time, begins with an article by William Stringfellow, a layman, who attacks Berton's brand of humanism for being too easy on the Church. He proceeds to make a devastating case against Christendom but, nevertheless, one which is so tough-minded and so compassionate in its premises and approach as to make in itself a very powerful case for the biblical way of looking at things.

Part Two on the Church's dialogue with the world it exists to love and serve is a discussion by three laymen: Patrick Watson, co-founder and host of the CBC television program "This Hour Has Seven Days"; Monica Furlong, the brilliant English journalist and, surely, the liveliest and most delightful writer on Church affairs extant; and John Wilkins, assistant editor of the oecumenical review, *Frontier*.

Part Three turns to the problem of faith and its content as seen by the Eugene Fairweather, Keble Professor of Divinity at Trinity College, Toronto, an official Anglican observer at the Second Oecumenical Council of the Vatican and a member of the Committee of Ten for discussion of Church union; and two controversial bishops, John Robinson of Woolwich, author of *Honest to God* and *The New Reformation?*; and James Pike of California, who seems to have been involved in almost every experiment or adventure the Episcopal Church has been engaged in during the past dozen years.

Part Four, "Other Quarters Heard From," includes essays by Peter Berger, a sociologist and author of *The Precarious Vision*; by Thomas Roberts, a Jesuit archbishop; and by Emil Fackenheim the rabbi and University of Toronto philosopher. Part Five is an imaginative and prophetic essay by the German-born Anglican priest Werner Pelz, and his wife Lotte, authors of a protest against religion in the name of Christianity, *God is No More*.

The book concludes with a statement by Pierre Berton written nine months after the publication of *The Comfortable Pew*. It is here not just as a matter of courtesy and the debating custom that gives the mover of a motion the opportunity of summing up, but to express the intention and hope that this book will be only one contribution to a continuing dialogue among many persons and points of view.

The other major contributors are my wife, Elizabeth Kilbourn, Michael Creal of York University, formerly general secretary of the Church's Department of Religious Education and Ernest Harrison, also of the Department and author of *Let God Go Free*, who were the two chief instigators in the commissioning both of Pierre Berton's book and this response to it.

I should particularly like to express my thanks to Michael Creal and Ernest Harrison and their staff, and to Philip Jefferson, editor of the Church's new curriculum, whose help has been crucial, continual, and invaluable at every stage in the preparation of this book. I should add, however, that the entire responsibility for the contents belongs not to the Church or its Department but to the editor. The decisions for which they are responsible (as in the case of *The Comfortable Pew*) was to commission one person to prepare a book and to give him complete freedom to do it as he saw fit.

This is not to say that I have tried to put together a book of essays whose viewpoint corresponded to my own. I do find myself in complete accord with the two articles in the prologue and nearly so with certain other essays, such as those by William Stringfellow and Monica Furlong. But I disagree strongly with some aspects of the approach or argument in several contributions. Peter Berger's brilliant article, for example, seems to me to come too close to insisting that Christians must choose between agreeing with Cardinal Ottaviani (or his Protestant equivalent) and giving up the biblical faith and the Church completely.

The book attempts to include a variety of positions – at least from among writers with experience and knowledge of the biblical way of looking at things. But, in choosing essay contributors, there was no attempt to achieve an even balance among all major opinions and groups – of Canadian Anglicans, of Jews and Christians generally, or of anybody else. Many important viewpoints are not represented at all, simply because they did not seem to me to be as vital or as interesting as others that are represented. I do particularly regret the absence from this book of a number of Canadian writers (who either could not participate or whose potential topics would have duplicated something already planned for), and of H. A. Williams of Trinity College, Cambridge, whose book *The True Wilderness* is one of the most appealing and profound works of popular theology I have read in a long time. What unity there is in this symposium must be found mainly in its subject matter and in the pattern and sequence of topics and approaches. In the end, of course, the general character of the book cannot help reflecting the editor's own prejudices about what matters most. To that extent this book represents the bias of someone who is Methodist in background and enthusiasm, Anglican by adoption, Catholic in doctrine of Church and Sacraments; who believes most things and doubts everything; sees the biblical faith as the best antidote for idolatry; regards the Church as a place for being vulnerable rather than safe, for celebration rather than constriction, for moral disarmament rather than judgement, for acceptance and reconciliation and openness to improbable connections rather than fine distinctions and precise definitions and ringing pronouncements; and who believes that Christianity, for the time being, is better understood as the main question put rather than a set of answers given – though answers there are, for those who will listen, in the holding to that hope that exists beyond hopelessness on the far side of longing and despair.

WILLIAM KILBOURN
*Toronto*
*November, 1965*

*William Kilbourn is professor of humanities at York University, Toronto and a member of the Anglican Church of Canada's Board of Religious Education. Author of three books on Canadian history,* The Firebrand, *winner of two national awards,* The Elements Combined, *and* The Making of the Nation, *he has also written articles, reviews, and television scripts on history, biography, the arts, and the Church.*

# THE RESTLESS CHURCH

# PROLOGUE

*Elizabeth Kilbourn is a writer, broadcaster, and art critic. A professor's wife and mother of five children, she is a member of the inner city parish of Holy Trinity in downtown Toronto.*

*Michael Creal is professor in charge of the Humanities program in Atkinson College, York University, and is developing several new projects in the University's centre for continuing education. As head of the Anglican Church's Department of Religious Education until 1965, he was responsible for starting a revolution in many aspects of the Church's life, including the New Curriculum and the training of church leaders. He was also responsible for the commissioning of* The Comfortable Pew.

# 1 A CONFESSION

I guess I was about the first person to be freed by *The Comfortable Pew*. Not by the book itself, nor by its author, but by the occasion of its writing. After all, I had read Tillich and Robinson and Bonhoeffer for myself and thrown them across the room in fury. *The Comfortable Pew* would certainly have been no better. For me, like most people I know, books are no substitute for personal encounter.

But while *The Comfortable Pew* was still work in progress, Pierre Berton met every Friday noon during the winter of 1963-64 in my living room with various clergymen from the Anglican church; the sessions would start abruptly with Pierre asking, "Well, what do you guys mean by God?" or "Do you really believe all that stuff in the Creeds?" I found that with such a large and articulate ally, I was brave enough to give vent to all the frustrations and irritations and plain downright disgust which I felt about the institutional church in Canada, A.D. 1964.

But once the hostility had bubbled up and been spewed out; once the act of destruction of the old order had been accomplished in my own mind; and the debris of pseudo-Gothic attitudes, archaic language, the fusty pomposity of solemn high matins, and the petty narrow moral standards lay in ruins around my feet; then what?

I began to look around me at the society I was so convinced that the Church had nothing to say to. It became apparent that Pierre's clarion call for updated attitudes to sex and war and business seemed like a little boy whistling in the dark, and that his final cry for a strong new Messiah betrayed a dependency as great as that of which he accused the clergy. I saw around me everywhere people who were desolate and isolated, mirroring with agonizing clarity the separation I found within myself. All the sturdy efforts of the humanitarian liberal I applauded and supported. But they are, after all, only brave and desperate footholds on the cliff of survival. I saw the terrible world-wide split of ideologies, of race against race, of rich against poor, the bitter separation of generation from generation, of sex from sex, the spectacle of radicals and conservatives at daggers drawn, even within the discipline of the Christian Church itself. I saw friends leap to suicide or drown themselves in alcohol or incessant sexual adventures. I saw others taken to the wards of psychiatric hospitals. At meetings, in the midst of intense discussions whether to reconvene on the third or fourth Monday, the masks would drop for a fleeting instant, and the pain and emptiness and loneliness reveal themselves. I saw men drive themselves with work, commit themselves totally to institutional structures, drug themselves with obsessive ideas; I saw women lose themselves in their children or charity or the politics of culture, things which, in Harry Williams' telling phrase, are like plastic flowers decorating a wilderness.

I suddenly realized in anguish that though I possessed all that the world rightly calls good – husband, children, friends, comfort, even a newspaper column with my picture at the top – I was not one of the ninety-nine sheep safely in the fold. I was the hundreth sheep clinging to a cliff overhanging the abyss in the dark night, with nobody hearing my cries, or, if they did, powerless to help.

And I was not alone. How many times in a darkened bar have I heard human beings confess that they can't feel love? Or that life is meaningless or flat or just plain hell. What about all the masks and defences and status symbols we parade around to hide from each other that paralyzing insecurity beneath? How does a church which claims that God is love say anything to a generation which not only cannot believe in God, but is terrified of love as well.

Perfect love casts out fear, said St. John, but it is more obvious that perfect fear banishes love. Think of the scholar building his life-proof wall of learned articles, the monographs of impeccably high academic standard, so that the frightened little boy within could never be glimpsed; the TV personality always on to bigger and better shows, so no one would suspect the hideous emptiness at the core; the professional flagellators of society turning their verbal whips on others to disguise their own self-hate; the dedicated members of institutions and upholders of moral standards terrified of facing their own desperate dependency; the perennial cynic protecting himself against the paralyzing agony of disappointment; and worst of all, the prisoner of the dogma of fashion in ideas and life styles, living in the cultural and intellectual world of Ins and Outs.

Surely, surely this is not all we were meant to be? In my rage and fury I cursed God. I demanded that the sneaky bastard show himself. And then in my pain, I discovered something about the parable of the Good Samaritan. Those people propped up by position and status and professional skills and intellectual fashion designing – in other words, most of the world's good and successful people – those people are not free enough to notice. Like the priest and the Levite, they pass by on the other side. The person who can bind up the wounds and pour in oil and wine is the Samaritan, the one who has suffered and had his own wounds bound. God did not come to me through a mystical experience, but through a human being, a neighbour, an agent of His love, paradoxically, a parish priest.

Paul van Buren's definition of Easter as the event which makes Christ's freedom contagious makes total sense to me. But the contagion of Christ's freedom must be caught from a carrier, and that carrier must himself be open to experience daily the agony of crucifixion and the glorious liberation of resurrection.

The Church for me is no longer an institution which demands my acceptance of certain abstractions, hallowed by history or decree. After all, I may or may not accept intellectually those abstractions, but they are only defence mechanisms, until I can accept them at the most primitive depths of my feelings. The Church I know is a small community of human beings who have caught the contagion of Christ's freedom and among whom I can be accepted for myself as I am: all of them ministers who, with their own wounds bound, are free to go out into society, sensitive to the cries of other humans in their multitudinous needs. I cannot forget that the first person who encountered Jesus risen was not Peter, the man of action, or John the intellectual, or James the organizer, but a weeping needy woman whose only resource was persistent love.

I do not say that I have emerged from my *Purgatorio*, but I do not doubt that, just as for St. Teresa, the interior castle is there for me to explore and take possession of. I hear St. Augustine's words "Seek for yourself, Betty; search for your own true self.

He who seeks shall find – but marvel and joy, he will not find himself, he will find God, or if he finds himself, he will find himself in God." And my ultimate concern is that search, that restless and insistent demand to take possession of those interior mansions of myself, and finding at last myself in Love, I will be free, in so far as I love and accept myself, to love and accept my neighbour.

## Michael Creal

## 2   A DECLARATION

Most human beings live with a depressing measure of unreality in their lives, performing many roles in which they have no investment and going through many motions with little commitment. Ironically, the Church, the only institution which exists precisely to be the setting where realities are faced and Reality is found, has become in our age typically the place where realities are avoided and emptiness is found. (Sometimes that emptiness is confused with religion or God, which is one reason why the stock of both words is so low at the moment.) If it were a standard of the Church's life that it was not only legitimate but mandatory to deal with what really bothered people, what really excited people, and what really mattered in the life of our society, it would soon be discovered that elements of the Christian tradition which had long been obscured under theological vocabulary and religious convention would come alive. Dimensions of truth would be disclosed which illuminated the very central issues of contemporary life.

If the Church is to be the instrument of Christ's ministry in the final years of this century, it will need to find ways of enabling its membership to perceive those realities in their own lives and in the life of society around them which point to that Reality which underlies all things and which is inexhaustibly creative and redemptive. The Church has no business shoring up the strength of its traditional institutional life, no business seeking any kind of privilege or favour or special treatment, no business attacking the valid achievements of secular culture. To shake itself loose from all these patterns, to rediscover the meaning of its corporate life and ministry, to enable its membership to find their participation in the ministry of Christ – until their ministry is in fact identified as the Church – to work towards such a renewal of the central radical mission of the Church as the servant of God and man, this is the path of life for the Church today. Pierre Berton's unwillingness to see the Church as anything other than the hierarchy is in fact a symptom of the corrupt state of the institution. Perhaps the clearest test of significant reform in the life of the Church will be the degree to which the word "Church" comes to be identified, not just with bishops and clergy, but with the total *laos*, bishops and clergy included.

The present institutional form may persist for many years but the longer it persists without changing, the more brittle and un-real it will become. Because of it, the central authentic tradition of "new life" which the Church has proclaimed and in some measure reflected through the centuries has been totally obscured for millions of people in our own generation. The test which now faces church members – laity quite as much as clergy – is whether or not it is possible to break out of the present structures of con-ventional middle-class religion; to face the theological issue of change boldly in vigorous, open, and creative debate; and, most important of all, to find and fulfill a kind of ministry which is genuinely contemporary and authentically Christian. To the degree that the Church in the parish (or in any other form it may take) becomes the context in which people can begin to face the full dimensions of their own lives, their own needs, their own worth, their own immense creative powers, to that degree will the Church begin to function as it is meant to.

---

# ONE

# THE SOCIAL AND MORAL ISSUES:
# HAS THE CHURCH ABDICATED?

---

*William Stringfellow is a practising attorney and a partner in a New York law firm. An Episcopalian who joined the staff of the East Harlem Protestant parish, he has spent much time working on behalf of underprivileged people who needed help and were not getting it. He is probably best known for his participation in the civil rights movement and for such books as* My People is the Enemy *and* Instead of Death.

*Ernest Harrison of the Anglican Church of Canada's Department of Religious Education is the author of a number of detective stories and such theological works as* Let God Go Free. *A former parish priest in Quebec, he suggested, when appointed to the Department in 1963, that Pierre Berton be asked to take a candid look at the Church and write about what he saw. He is presently helping to develop a new approach to education in the Canadian Church.*

# 1  THE CASE AGAINST CHRISTENDOM AND THE CASE AGAINST PIERRE BERTON

### A  THE CASE AGAINST CHRISTENDOM

Pierre Berton tells the Protestant churches very clearly what the world thinks of them. They appear, more than anything else, pathetic. This is a proposition with which it is difficult for a Christian to quarrel.

As a churchman, I judge the general thrust of Berton's assault on the contemporary North American churches both fair and warranted. My first complaint is that a far more trenchant, urgent, and embarrassing case could have been made. Berton damns by faint criticism. I will state some objections to his basic assumptions presently, but first consider his case against Christendom, taking each of the moral issues specifically treated in his book.

*The Self-righteous "Isms"* / Berton poses the issue of identifying national and ideological causes with the will of God, asking if God really is partisan in the conflicts familiar to the nations of the world. The issue is far broader than he appreciates. He relies mainly upon statements during the First World War of the public authorities and the ecclesiastical establishment on both sides invoking God as an ally, but rarely mentions that much the same thing took place in the Second World War when, for example, in Germany an esoteric apology for Nazism as the fulfillment of God's law was made, and most of the clergy either openly endorsed or tacitly acquiesced in the Nazi cause. Meanwhile, Churchill and Roosevelt – if not Stalin – repeatedly reassured their peoples of God's favour for the Allies, and the churches for the most part echoed the same sentiment.

But there are many other situations, apart from war, where nations regard customs and institutions as ordained by God and their own nationalistic and ideological self-interests as favoured by God over those of their enemies. Thus, in the Cold War, especially in the United States, the ordinary citizens have been brainwashed by political representatives, military leaders, the public media, and churchly spokesmen in the notion that the "free world" is defending itself against "godless" Communism, the inference being that God is somehow enshrined in "the American way of life" and that the political victory of Communism in the world would somehow mark the end of God's existence or, at least, reduce His influence. At the same time, there have been many instances, notably in the so-called peace movement in the Communist nations, where the ecclesiastical authorities have presumed to give God's endorsement to the aims of world Communism.

Among certain classes and races, too, it is common for particular self-interests to be identified with God's will. The *laissez-faire* capitalists so prominent among North American Protestant denominations argue this way, while, at the same time, many democratic socialists in Britain and North America equate their own economic and social views with the idea of a Christian society. The churches conforming to Southern white society in the United States are attended and supported by many who earnestly believe that segregation embodies God's law, and their kin in the Union of South Africa have accomplished all sorts of theological contortions to press this doctrine to its ultimate absurdities. In the era of the social gospel, many of the clergy, moved, I trust, by sincere compassion for the victims of depression, naively supposed that the aspirations of the labour revolution were an approximation of the Kingdom of God on earth. Doctrinaire pacifists perennially suffer from a delusion that theirs is the literal way of the Lord. Idealists and opportunists of all sorts (remembering that there may not be much distinction between idealism and opportunism in any of their forms) constantly impute to their own partisanship the sanction of God's approval.

Interestingly enough, Pierre Berton, while launching his diatribe against those in the First War who claimed God for their own causes, himself admits *his* conviction that God does prefer Western democracy to other forms of society. The point which he entirely overlooks, in his otherwise well-placed complaint against the identification of ideological or nationalistic causes with God's will, is that the Gospel of Christ authorizes no identification with *any* ideology or nation, whatever its character or content, whatever the age or circumstances, whether they seem evil or benign, since *all* such identifications are *inherently* idolatrous. Any such identification demeans the Gospel by making God the mere servant of national or racial or institutional or ideological survival.

The churches, especially the ecclesiastical authorities of the churches, are constantly tempted to conform in this fashion to the world. Evidently, for example, this was a grave issue in the early Church in Galatia; in any event it is no recent problem in the Church.

There is not, there has never been, and there never can be any actual or ideal order of secular life which satisfies the conscience of the Gospel.

Thus, there is never a nation or ideology or worldly institution of any kind explicitly identified as God's will for the world. The only society in this world which represents God's will for this world is, in truth, the Church of Christ. The Church, in this sense distinguished from the existing churchly institutions, is that community already living in unity within itself and in reconciliation with all men and all things, in which all worldly distinctions of nation or race or class or ideology or the like are transcended. The Church, in this sense, is invariably in a posture of witnessing *against* the nations and the ideologies and all other forms of society familiar to the world, because the Church is the image of the true society – the holy nation, the new creation – living already in the midst of the old and decadent and transient societies of the world. Far from ever lending uncritical allegiance and endorsement to the self-interest of any nation or ideology, from assuring any nation or ideology of its self-righteousness in the sight of God, Christians are called *always* to expose and protest the idolatry of nation and the worship of ideology. They must do so in the name of the insight and experience they have suffered in the true society which is the Church of Christ.

*Nuclear War* / It is precisely because the churches have lost so much a sense of the Church as a holy nation standing over against all nations that they have been, as Berton properly emphasizes, so timid in addressing the issues of nuclear power: both the use of nuclear weapons in war and the threat which nuclear capability has become in international politics. As Berton recognizes, the initial silence and apathy of the churches toward the holocaust in Japan is dramatized all the more by the belatedness of recent pronouncements of some of the church assemblies opposing the use of nuclear weapons in war. The churches ventured such a stand only after it was popularly safe to do so and after policies of the major nuclear powers had changed to accommodate some limitation in the testing of weapons. That change in national policies, on the part of the Soviet Union and the United States in particular, came, however, only when each had assembled such massive nuclear arsenals of temporal destructiveness that to add to them would be absurd. The world can only be blown up once, and there is little point in being capable of blowing it up more than once. That makes the recent condemnations by the churches not only tardy but a travesty of Christian witness.

Let that not cause any to lose sight of the witness made right from the time of Hiroshima by some individual Christians as well as such groups as the Quakers, the Catholic Workers, and the Fellowship of Reconciliation. In other words, at any given time on any specific issue, one must not assume uncritically that the ecclesiastical authorities speak for the Church of Christ in this world. Saint Paul was frequently concerned to make such a distinction. He discerned the institutional churches conforming to the world and denounced that conformity in the name of Christ and His Church. And, surely, Kierkegaard exercised a similar vocation to witness against what the ecclesiastical establishment of his day stood for. Who shall it be said spoke for the Church of Christ in the Nazi era in Germany – the churches there who withdrew into religious pietism and theological pedantics? Or the confessing Church movement and those identified with it, like Barth who was exiled or Bonhoeffer who was executed? There is, in other words, by God's grace, a prophetic office and tradition in the Church, as there always has been, and there are at large among the churches some prophets today. If few of them are elevated to the episcopacy or delegated to churchly councils, that does not vitiate their witness but only lends it urgency.

Berton links the problem of nuclear weapons with concept of the just war. My own conscience as a Christian is that there is simply no such thing as just war, nor has there been at any time, anywhere, not even, to use an example otherwise dear to the heart, the American Revolution. But the matter is not for me to judge. I am not an ideological pacifist, nor do I believe that a Christian may never be involved in war. I affirm the Christians who fought in the anti-Nazi underground, among many other instances that might be cited. I am only saying that how a particular war is regarded is a matter only disclosed in God's own judgement and Christians are not called upon to second guess that judgement. The Christian, rather, is always called to decide and act in the immediate circumstances in which he *is* – in fidelity to the Gospel, and, therefore, free from any concern for the preservation of his own life and free to trust the judgement of his action to God. He must be aware that his failure to act is itself an action of consequence, and yet he must be conscious of the moral ambiguity of all human decision.

Just as there are no just wars, as far as I can know, there is also no such thing as a just peace(using peace, now, only to mean the cessation of military hostilities). If nuclear war is a particular offence to Christians, because it threatens the very existence of mankind on earth, so, for instance, are poverty and disease and hunger whenever they exist where there is also the capacity to banish them. In war the power of death is at work in this world aggressively and notoriously. But it is also present and militant when there is no war, and the Christian concern extends just as much to that fact. Let the witness be heard against the use of nuclear weapons, but let it also be heard for the use of the resources of the earth and for the genius of men against the power of death in times called peace.

*Race* / The superficiality of Berton's analysis of the contemporary churches is perhaps clearest in his consideration of the racial crisis, at least in the United States. The indictment of the American churches for supporting a racist *status quo* for four centuries is wholly justified, but this can be much more amply documented than just by the practice of segregation in congregations and in church-related institutions. For generations, up to the present day, the vast majority of churchly bodies have invested their endowments in business enterprises which have and do uphold racism in one form or another in advertising, merchandising, hiring, promotions, job security, and the like. Only one major white Protestant national mission board, for example, has even seriously raised the question of the social consequences of its investments, while an illustrous university, originally founded by one of the churches in the colonial era, is a principal stockholder of the private utility corporation which dominates the economy of one of the deep South states most notorious for its die-hard segregationist stance. In hundreds of communities across the United States, in congregations which pride themselves in welcoming Negroes into their worship and life and which have taken public positions in support of integration, it has nót yet even occurred to the conscience of their trustees that the way they invest the parish's money may be inconsistent with their concern for racial equality.

Meanwhile, the tardy, but impressive involvement in the past few years of the main-line white churches in the civil rights movement, notably in the March on Washington and in the events at Selma, Alabama, is still marred by paternalism and condescension. It has not been enough to exorcise from the mentality of most American white church-goers the attitudes of white supremacy in which they have been reared in both the North and the South for generations. Even at the points of direct commitment and action, the churches have been following the world. It was more than eight years *after* the historic turning point in public policy – in the Supreme Court's school desegregation decision – that the major white denominations began to move.

But if the indictment of the churches should be more severe than Berton has made it, the essence of his argument is accurate and fair. He should not have ignored, however, the renewal of the Church which has taken place, because of the racial crisis in America, in those churches which have been traditionally Negro. The freedom movement, particularly in the South, had its inspiration as well as its organic roots in the Negro congregations. A host of civil rights leaders have sprung from the same origins. In the midst of the racial struggle, the Negro congregation has become the meeting place and, indeed, a place of reconciliation, between black men and white men and among Catholics and almost every variety of Protestant. Someone remarked during the trouble in Selma that the gathering of Christians there was the most authentic oecumenical event since Pentecost. Whether it was quite that I do not venture to say, but it surely was the most authentic oecumenical event that has ever happened in the United States. If the white churches have been slow to move, if in many aspects of their existence they still unwittingly support racism, if many white church people remain apathetic, the Church of Christ has, nonetheless, been mightily renewed in the racial crisis. And the *locus* of that renewal is significantly, though not exclusively, in the Negro sects and denominations.

Berton attempts to lump together the American racial struggle with the discrimination and rejection endured in America and in many other places by Indians and Orientals and Mexicans and Puerto Ricans. No doubt there are important similarities, say, for the Japanese who were relocated during the Second World War in Canada and in the United States, or for Puerto Ricans who have migrated to the urban jurisdictions on the continent, or for those imported from Mexico and elsewhere as migrant labourers, or for the Indians imprisoned on reservations. Yet whatever similarities exist cannot mitigate or dismiss the uniqueness of the situation of the American Negro. No other group save the Negro bears an inheritance of slavery and, equally significant, as to no other people does the dominant white society itself have such an inheritance. It is not just that Negroes and whites differ racially and that the whites have shunned the Negroes in the way that they have rejected and exploited the differences of language or culture or origin or custom of other ethnic groups; but rather that *both* Negroes and whites now confront the trauma of being absolved from the idea (inherited from the times of slavery) that Negroes are not human beings. That is a terrible and unique dimension of the present racial crisis in America, and one which cannot be evaded because Orientals or Indians or Latin Americans are in various other ways discriminated against and deprived.

Perhaps the most serious complaint against the major white churches in the matter of race is that when finally stirred to make a pronouncement or become directly active, these churches have been content merely to echo the secular ethics of humanism concerning brotherhood, equality, and freedom. These are splendid ethics, and they are most influential in the democratic tradition. But they do not express the peculiar concern of the Gospel, and it is that concern that the churches are called to bespeak. Racism, in any of its forms, raises for the Christian Church the issue of the meaning of Baptism. It raises, in other words, a most intimate question about the nature of the Church as such.

Baptism is, I know, a most profaned sacrament. It is so often observed as some private and family ritual having no particular significance for the world. But that is not, theologically, what Baptism is at all. Baptism is the sacrament of the reconciliation of all mankind in Jesus Christ. Baptism is, thus, an event in which it is vouchsafed, by God's action, that this person, now baptized, enters into an estate of reconciliation within himself, with all other men and, indeed, with all things, transcending, here and now, all worldly distinctions of class or education or age or sex or nationality or race. Thus, wherever Baptism is honoured and celebrated for what it is, there the Church is; and the Church lives as a visible community embracing within itself all sorts and conditions of men – not for the sake of democracy, but because, in fact, all men have been reconciled in Christ, and because the Church is the historic and corporate and (if you will) political witness to that reconciliation. Thus the man who professes to be a Christian and who is *not now* living in reconciliation with other men of a different race is disavowing in his actual life his own Baptism. And so, too, the churches which are not *in fact* living now as communities of reconciliation transcending worldly distinctions like race in their everyday existence are churches which are apostate. It is Baptism of which the churches should be speaking, if they are to be Christian in their witness in the racial crisis and not merely echoing the prevailing public ethics of Society.

*The Ethics of Good Business* / Berton sees the indifference and conformity of the churches in social witness as related to the separation of the practice of religion from the realities of practical life. But once again his criticism does not go far enough. The churches have not only failed to raise substantive ethical issues in the realms of commerce and industry, they have not only neglected the working classes; they have yet to address significantly the emerging problems posed by cybernetics and automation. They have ignored the legions of people being made unemployable by the impact of advanced technology upon society, and those living in early retirement or other forms of en-forced leisure.

The silence of the churches about the multiple issues wrought by automation is especially ironical for those churches fond of preaching abstinence in areas of personal morality. In these private matters abstinence is at least recognized as a viable ethical option: not everything within the inclination or access of men should be pursued. But should not a parallel principle be acknowl-edged in public affairs? Does every discovery or invention within men's capability need to be uncritically put to use? As for each technological development in contemporary mass society, should not the churches be asking what its discernible consequences for human life in society may be? Should they not raise the issue as to whether or not certain new processes should be used at all? In fact, of course, the nations in the nuclear test ban treaty have honoured in part such a principle by concluding that just because men are capable of destroying the planet, it does not follow that they must hasten to do so. Yet in the commercial sectors of society the idea seems to be that whatever can be invented should be uncritically regarded as a blessing and used with all deliberate haste, without serious consideration of the human consequences of that use.

Perhaps this failure of the churches even to mention the option of abstention in the commercial sphere is related to a serious theological error with which the churches in North America have been enamoured for a long time – long before the age of automa-tion. That is a crude doctrine of justification by works in which a man's moral significance is thought to be measured by his acquisition and control of property. This notion, still preached and propagated widely in the churches, has its origins, I suggest, in the idea popular at the beginning of the Industrial Revolution that work in itself is a virtue, and that the man who is enterpris-ing, competitive, and financially successful is somehow morally superior to other men. Theologically, the image of the "self-made man" attributes ultimate moral worth to the acquisition of prop-erty. Nowadays, when wealth (like poverty) is more often a matter of inheritance than individual initiative, and when control of property is far more socially significant than outright ownership of property, the doctrine has been transmuted to attach to the mere holding of property or of the symbols of property.

The idea that acquisition of property justifies a man absurdly overlooks how much those who are affluent depend directly and indirectly upon the poor for their prosperity. It sacrifices human rights to property rights and abandons society to be governed by an ethic of greed. In Christian terms, it is an abomination to the insight of the Gospel – which makes it clear that men are only justified by God's free initiative and love.

The notion that a man's moral significance is measured by his acquisition and control of property, whatever its historic origins, remains exceedingly popular today. If anything, its popularity increases as resistance to social change hardens among the prosperous and the privileged; for example in the civil rights struggle in the United States, they see that social change would diminish their economic and political power and their social dominance. The Goldwater presidential campaign in 1964, whatever else may be said of it, was in part a mobilization of the propertied classes, and those who identify with those classes (even if they have little property of their own) to re-establish the precedence of property rights over human rights as the fundamental ideological structure of society. The religious fervor and moral zeal of the Goldwaterites both during the campaign and since is understandable and appropriate too; for their basic commitment is to property as an idol in whose service a man is, in an ultimate sense, justified. In its mature form as an idol, property becomes a symbol, not only of his moral superiority in this world, but also the means by which his life gains moral significance which survives his death. Thus the man of property who dies and leaves a large estate achieves, it is supposed, a kind of immortality.

This idolatry of property, like all idolatries, ends, of course, in nihilism, that is, in the worship of death, since men die, and property and whatever property can accomplish dies also.

Where is the witness of the churches against such idolatry? Certainly not in the paternalism of mission work among the poor and disadvantaged both at home and abroad. Certainly not, as Berton points out, in the neglect of industrial workers or the failure to render a Christian critique of business ethics. Certainly not in the issues of automation and cybernetics in a mass urbanized society, because, with but a half dozen exceptions on the whole continent of North America, the churches remain silent about those problems. Certainly not in those congregations where, for example, building funds are initiated mainly in order to provide people with some "church work" to do, or in those where maintaining the churchly enterprise as a property institution is itself the operative morality dominating the existence of the parish. Certainly not in those denominations where prudent investment rather than conscious social witness governs the use of endowment and income. Certainly not, in other words, where the churches in one sense or another are, intentionally or insensitively, themselves idolatrous of property.

Yet there *is* a witness in Christ's Church against the idolatry of property and all that goes with it. It is, surely, among those Christians yet dispersed in this world who live in the freedom of voluntary poverty, among all sorts and conditions of men, celebrating the truth that since nothing they have, including their very lives, is their own, they are at liberty to give away whatever they have as a sacrament of Christ's own gift of Himself to the whole world.

*Pre-packaged Morality* / One premise of Berton's discussion of sexual morality is that a "sexual revolution" exists which the churches are ignoring while still reciting a "pre-packaged" code of sexual morals no longer realistic or relevant.

I, for one, doubt that the actualities of sexual behaviour in contemporary North American society have the dignity of a revolution – if that is supposed to mean that there is now, suddenly, a greater incidence than in earlier times or in other societies of premarital intercourse, adolescent sexual experimentation, incest, homosexuality, pornography, extra-marital promiscuity, or public obscenity. I don't think the watusi is really any more "sexy" than the minuet. I doubt that adultery is more prevalent now than it was, say, in the time of slavery in the American South. I would be surprised if it turned out that boys in urban slums masturbate more often than rural lads did before the First World War or entertain very different sexual fantasies. Sunday School adolescents may not confide the secrets of their sexual behaviour to their ministers but neither do most adults, and, besides, many of the clergy are not exactly straight-laced or straightforward in their sexual conduct. What is clearly different today, as compared with other times, is the revolution in communications. When six boys, all sons of prominent, church-going families form a club to seduce girls and are finally charged with multiple rape – as happened recently in one city – it reached the front pages of virtually every newspaper on the continent. And obviously, along with modern communications which cause such an incident to have great notoriety rather than remain home-town news, there is the revolution in obtaining and disseminating data pertaining to sexual activity. The Kinsey reports are examples of this. Medical examination of students in most public schools now furnish information about the prevalence of venereal diseases, and, thus, some index to the prevalence of sexual relations among young people. I am dubious if such data had been assembled and kept in earlier periods that it would indicate significantly different sexual behaviour than that evidenced by such data now available.

But whether or not there is a "sexual revolution" today, Berton is substantially justified in saying that the churches are still advocating a moral code for sexual conduct that is antique, unrealistic, and lacking in compassion. However, I believe that he avoids the central problem. Where the churches are amiss, specifically in the nurture of the young, is in setting before adolescents an ideal of "Christian marriage" which is asserted to be the only appropriate context of sexual relations. Theologically this is objectionable because there is no such thing as "Christian marriage." On the contrary, marriage is, Biblically speaking, a fallen estate, known only in this existence, afflicted with the ambiguity of all fallen relationships. Such a marriage between two Christians may be consecrated and sacramentalized within the Church, of course, just as daily work, or any other relationship common to life in this world, but there is no "higher" or "better" estate of marriage for Christians than for anybody else. Yet the children are taught in the churches all too often that there is such an ideal, which they should covet for themselves and which, if they do not attain it (*it has never been attained*), will somehow impair their relationship with God and thwart their personal fulfillment. This emphasis on so-called Christian marriage in the churches is in fact a reversion to Greek mythology and is not defensible theolo-

gically. Perhaps worse than that, it is not defensible psycho-
logically. Here they are – clergy and parents and teachers – talking
to adolescents about marriage at a time and in a society in which
marriage, because of the necessities of university training and
military service and professional qualifications, is not an option
for another decade. Instead, they might try to face the real,
sexual problems that are familiar (and always have been) to
adolescent life. What the churches should be doing is bringing
into open, frank, and, hopefully, compassionate discussion the
real issues youngsters immediately confront: petting, masturba-
tion, the facts about venereal disease, homosexuality, and, perhaps most of all, sexuality as a natural and inherent dimension of
*all* human relationships – not only husband and wife, but parent
and child, friend and friend, youth and adult, male and female. If
that were the focus of the church's ministry in the realm of sex,
more young people might be mature enough to enter into and
maintain an adult marriage with fidelity. If that were done, the
churches would not need to cling to simplistic "pre-packaged"
codes, old or new, and would begin to care for people as persons
who are, among other things, sexual beings. If that were the case,
sex would not be so confined to the back seats of automobiles or
the dark corners of the mind; it would become mentionable in the
sanctuaries of the churches and honoured there and elsewhere for
the gift of God which it is.

B    THE CASE AGAINST PIERRE BERTON

*How will the Church Survive?* / The premise of Berton's book
appears to be that the Church, by exposure to criticism, including
justifiable complaints, will somehow be insured continuance for,
at least, the remainder of the century. That is an un-Biblical view,
and a morbid one as well. That is a form of flagellation (a recur-
rent ailment of Protestants); it is, theologically, a kind of justification by works in reverse. *The Comfortable Pew*, it seems, is
commissioned and its critique commended to churchly folk under
pain of punishment (the threat that the Church may die in this
century) if not heeded.

But no mere infidelity of those who profess to be Christians,
no mere compromise or complicity with the world on the part

of churchly institutions, no mere complacency or opportunism on the part of the ecclesiastical authorities can threaten the extinction of Christ's Church or refute the veracity of the Gospel of Christ. No doubt some churches can only survive if emancipated from such infidelities. No doubt, too, that some sects and denominations now prosper just because of their betrayal of the Gospel. Neither of these facts assaying the survival of the churchly institutions, however, are decisive as to the life and survival of the Church as such.

According to St. Paul, in fact, falsehood and weakness within the precincts of the Church, just because they are so futile, serve only to magnify the reality of the Church in this world and to clarify the truth of the Gospel for this world.

The real constitution and existence of the Church depends upon a generous and patient dispensation of God toward human beings and institutions in this world, and the presence and future of the Church does not depend upon the faithfulness in word or deed of men or institutions. The life of the Church depends upon God's faithfulness to the world. The Church of Christ is, simply, a gift of God to the world; the Church survives in the world by the authenticity of that gift – by grace – and to that estate of the Church nothing can be added or taken away.

The relationship of apostasy to the survival of the Church is dramatized Biblically in the history of Israel. At the end of that saga, on the day when all of Israel had become apostate, on Good Friday, God remained faithful and Israel still lived, as it were, within the singular person of Christ Himself on the cross.

*Is the Gospel Essentially about Ethics?* / Pierre Berton regards the Gospel as essentially a system of ethical imperatives: his objection to the churches is only that they have departed from these ethics in one fashion or another and accommodated themselves too much to the ethics of the world. But the Gospel is not mainly about morals even though that may often be the main concern of the churches. The most cogent indictment of the churches which Berton's book actually makes is, in a sense, *himself* and his own Sunday School indoctrination in which he was misled, as so many others are, into supposing that the Gospel is just a radical ethical idealism which should be applied to practical affairs in the world today. Again and again and again Berton fails to distinguish between ethical idealism and voluntary love, between mere human moral insight and sacramental action in this world, between justice and grace, between the conflict of good and evil and the drama of death and resurrection.

*The Nostalgia for a New Saviour* / This is why the very end of Berton's book is so ambivalent. Here he has spent all this time arguing that the churches have been ethically compromised or, in some instances, ethically wrong – unfaithful in either instance, as he sees things, to the Gospel.

Then, he changes his plea. No longer does he say that the churches must somehow retrieve  the ethics which he prefers and which he identifies so readily with the Gospel.

In the end he says what is needed is not a recovery of "Christian" ethical imperative, but a "new Christ" Who would come again and Who would repeat in "His" ministry the very drama of Christ Himself.

It is an astonishing switch, and one wonders how typical it is. Berton himself acknowledges by his own nostalgia for Christ the fact – despite all of his complaints against the churches, whether legitimate or not – that what is needed is not some system of ethical imperatives but a witness to and an embodiment of the life of man reconciled within himself and to all things and all men. So Berton beseeches another "Christ" to come and to be for men the example of that reconciliation, even while admitting, as he does, that such a "One" who would come would be bound to be rejected, betrayed, and executed.

To that plea of Pierre Berton, all that I can say is: there is no urgency for "another Christ"; the Christ who has already come amongst us is for all men for all time. He is for *you*, He is for *me*, He is for *all* men everywhere. Wherever the Church which bears His name and ministry is alive (which I admit may not be everywhere), the Christ whom you long for is celebrated and made known to all the world *by* the love and service she gives to the world, though the world – though you – may not acknowledge as much.

## 2 THE IMMORALITY OF THE BIBLE

He was a sensitive man, a believer. No fanatic, no declaimer, no hater of other faiths, no hypocrite in the style of Pierre Berton's racketeering evangelist. He was gentle, sympathetic, and fun with children. The last time I met him was after his child had been buried, after he had refused to give permission for a blood transfusion. Today, the doctors would proceed without it, but in those days it was not easy, and time moved too fast. His child died. At the heart of the grief which nearly destroyed him, I detected no sense of responsibility, for God had ordained that there should be no devouring of blood, and had declared the law clearly in the Bible, his inerrable word.

My friend is not alone. There are still large, and apparently growing, numbers of Christians who accept the Bible as infallible at all points, only to be challenged at the peril of the critic. From this conviction spring conclusions and actions which, repugnant to many of us, seem inevitable to the believer. Reading his scriptures, he comes to the conclusion that we must segregate the skins of mankind; allow wives to die for lack of a hysterectomy; live in a mockery of a family for lack of a divorce; face intolerable burdens for lack of birth control; starve or suffer in prison for lack of psychological aid.

Nor is this attitude restricted to the unquestioning Christian. The Bible is often seen, by outsiders, as a book which makes pretensions to infallibility. Though they have parted company with religion and the Church, they still approach it as an oracle – one which they have disowned, to be sure, but an oracle none the less. They may even find themselves resentful when Christians demand the liberty to part company with it and to criticize its implications.

For there is so much to criticize, so much which gives pain and anguish. No matter how much you modernize the texts, re-tell, re-translate, delete, explain, and bowdlerize – there still remain certain hard, disturbing streaks that are impervious. The curiously arbitrary treatment of Cain and of Esau, or Adam and Eve (surely not a very offensive act they performed), the elevation of the arrogant Joseph, the blessing of the dishonest Jacob – such narratives can raise the hackles of anyone who resents cruelty or unfairness.

The stories, of course, can be dealt with in another way. We can soften them in commentary and sermon because they are stories, brilliant and incisively told for a purpose, and that purpose a deep and penetrating one. At it stands, the material may strike us as odd; but after all old stories are like that (as witness Grimm's grisly fairy tales), and we can detect what the writers were driving at, even when their detail makes us wriggle uncomfortably. We can remind ourselves that no actual human beings suffered precisely as described in Genesis; we are reading parables and fables. We can insist that when Jesus told a fable about a slave, he was not condoning slavery.

Yet, when we have done this, there remains the biblical material which is historical. What of the figures who were part of the pattern of early nomadic and settled life in Palestine? Once again, we can soften our hurt by reminding ourselves that such books as Chronicles have passed through the hands of narrow-minded editors who tested each man's actions by some hard-and-fast party line. Yet, having allowed for this, we are still faced with the inescapable accounting of bloodshed, horror, death, torture, and mutilation. Even when the narrative has been cushioned or injected with reverence, there persists the hard core of David's tyranny, the unreasonable and fantastically cruel treatment of the Canaanites, and Jael's appalling treachery – all offered as part of God's action. These incidents, and hundreds more, are presented as examples of the God of history working in the middle of world events. Directly working, because the murder of Sisera is explained as part of God's work, "for so God subdued the King of Canaan before the children of Israel." A strange God, with strange ways.

The New Testament, though the battles and cries of the tortured and dying are no longer described with gusto, continues to show this same cruel streak which offers so much for us to react against. There are tales involving hell fire and the eternal punishment of the disobedient. The bowels of Judas gush out. Ananias and Sapphira are stricken down when they sell their property and keep back a part for themselves, instead of passing over all the proceeds to the apostles. Not an action of unconditional generosity, but justification surely for no more than a rebuke and perhaps a concession that the apostles were asking a good deal. And yet they die a degrading and merciless death. Admittedly, God is not described as doing this directly, and their own guilt may have triggered their collapse, but it is a strangely disconcerting incident all the same; no wonder that "great fear came on all the Church." Then there are the chilling accounts in Revelation of the punishment of those who have sinned, an ultimate punishment devoid of compassion, not regretted by the saints, but apparently rejoiced in. These examples may quickly be multiplied by a mere turning of the pages.

The plea of this essay is that, when the Christian is faced with such incidents and cannot accept the biblical presentation or interpretation, that he be permitted, and even encouraged, to say so. As things stand, such permission is either not given or is not seen to be given. If a preacher declares that he thinks the Bible is not right at a certain point or on a particular issue, he quickly finds himself facing the charge of heresy. And this charge is not limited to those in authority or in the pew; it is in his own mind also. The worm bites away. The Bible is the Word of God. It may not be questioned. And what applies to the preacher, applies in different contexts and in different ways, to the layman.

Forced into a corner, he seeks an escape. Sometimes as the simplest solution, he rejects the whole of the Bible, for, if he rejects everything, then he rejects the particular issues which have hurt him. Or sometimes he simply ignores those issues which have proved difficult for him to accept. Or he explains them away with the help of commentaries. Or he offers other illustrations which offset the cruel ones, as if, in the realm of human relations, a cruel act were like an acid, to be neutralized by the alkali of a kindly one.

It is, perhaps, the second escape route – that of ignoring the awkward issues – which is followed by the North American Protestant. In general, he accepts the Golden Rule as the foundation stone of Christianity and sees his religion enshrined in the Victorian system of morality which is built into his ideal, though not actual, way of life. He has little difficulty in perceiving the

Christian faith as kindliness, middle-class virtue, and democracy. For him, therefore, the Bible must remain a closed book, heard only in extracts and in certain safe areas, such as lecterns and pulpits. When he is challenged with some of the uglier aspects of Bible teaching, he normally refuses to examine them deeply, leaving such problems to the minister, while he himself disclaims any responsibility for study or interpretation, pleading ignorance. At this point, he is joined by many of his Roman Catholic friends.

This is a tragic and unnecessary route to follow, as are all other escapes. For, in taking them, the Christian denies himself the privilege of coming to grips with the Bible. Once, however, the freedom to criticize has been conceded, then a giant step has been taken to grasping those forces in the Bible which guarantee life.

There is, in the first place, another streak which runs right through the Bible, the streak of acceptance and compassion. It starts way back in the fables, when an element of mercy enters Cain's punishment, or a rainbow appears in the sky; runs unobtrusively through the history books with their periodic acknowledgement that God is merciful; comes to a flood in the Prophets with their proclamation of God's dynamic concern for the poor and outcast; and pours into the New Testament with its unyielding premise that God is love.

Then there is the overwhelming fact that the Bible is seen by many Christians as a self-authenticating book. They do not accept it because the Church tells them to, or because society accepts it as such, or because they ought to, but because they discover in it the drama of creation. So far, I have spoken as if it were a set of streaks which we can examine separately, accept in pieces, or reject in pieces; and the freedom to do this is, I believe, important. At the same time, although the Bible is many books, and each book many writings of varying truth and quality, the Bible is also one book. *The* book, many would say truly.

This discovery is most naturally made when no sanctions are applied to the reader. Once permitted to read freely, with no preconceived commitment, he finds that he has in his hands a pulsing, living reality; not just a pious collection of religious lore, but a reality which moves beyond the bounds of the Church or the Faith. For we are in the presence of a surge of human love and beauty, cruelty and dismay, close relations and cruel separations, the force of the sexual act and the fear which pervades it, the magnificence of God and His meanness, His fierce truth and the petty acts of which He Himself repents, thoughtless giving and divine taking, soaring wisdom and pedestrian drivel, rounded organ music and shrill pipe, high philosophy and dogged literalism, heavy restrictions and unremitting freedoms, wit and boredom, priest and prophet, faith and unfaith – life itself.

At the heart of this unceasing, uncontrollable, and undisciplined life which is God, there is the constant immorality of the Bible, that immorality which is the life of any age, not least our own. The Bible has run counter to the morality of every generation in which it has been preached. Modern North American society, for example, values hard work; laziness is considered a vice, especially when accompanied by poverty. In these matters, the Bible presents no acceptable morality. Genesis describes work as a punishment, an apposite description. While Esau is hard at work, Jacob is making arrangements to steal his birthright. In Jesus' parables, there is some suggestion that work is useful (as with the five sensible virgins who prepare their lamps), but much to suggest that it is not overly admired. The men who look after their wives and perform their allotted tasks with their animals and property, are condemned, because they should have been at a party. The labourers who work only one hour in the vineyard are given as much as those who work all day, and receive it first. The dishonest bailiff is praised. The elder brother who works faithfully has to concede the fatted calf to the one who went off and had a good time. The sower works no harder on the seed which brings forth a hundred fold than on that which brings forth nothing. That those who serve the Lord may also work is not disputed, and Saint Paul felt no shame in being a tent-maker; but work in and of itself is not considered praiseworthy. Mary is supported, while the hard-working, faithful Martha is left to do the dirty work and, quite rightly, grumbles about it. Jesus came through to the leaders of society as a rebel, a drunkard, and a mocker of religion.

The immoral teaching is particularly significant because it raises problems, not only for those who agree, but more notably for those who are embarrassed by it. In every matter quoted in this chapter, there are other reasonable interpretations to be made, other slants to be detected, other valid conclusions to be reached. There are those who think that the elder brother was a better person than the prodigal, that their father acted despicably, that Victorian sexual morality is a sounder way of life than Abraham's, and that hard work is better than going to a party.

There is, therefore, no solution to be found to our biblical difficulties by simply selecting certain parts, and eliminating the rest. Whatever our agreements and disagreements, we can only meet the Bible if we take it as a whole; and this can only be done honestly when we have been given the unconditional freedom to accept or reject any of its parts. For the Bible accounts not only for the strengths of the Christian Church, but also in a sense for its weaknesses. It is neither perfect nor infallible, but living and creative. For better or worse, the Bible is our foundation document and we cannot escape it.

The Church remains an institution to arouse the wrath of the Bertons, a wrath which will always be well-based. For it is here in the Bible that we see the roots of our malaise, our hopelessness, and our meanness; our built-in cruelties which grind people to pulp in the name of the Lord, instilling guilt where there is no wrong, undermining humanity where there is no cause, and loading on indignities where God has given his greatest compliment, creation.

At the same time, neither we nor the Bertons can escape the wholeness of the foundation document, which absorbs and even transmutes the blackness. Because of its roots in the Bible, the Church is still that institution which guarantees, and is seen to guarantee, compassion and acceptance. The priest who refuses to help those in need is quickly condemned, where other members of society, including the Church's critics, are not held responsible. Why? Because the Church is seen as the home of compassion where the worlds of business, writing, and science are not. A bum comes to a big city like Toronto. What is he to do? His life has been drained from him by the coldness and cruelty of government and law at all levels; he has nothing left but his body and such dignity as he has been able to preserve. Where may he go for help? To those in society whom Berton praises as its Saviours — the science clubs, the agnostics' meeting places, the reporters' societies, the psychologists' guilds?

Perhaps, and such possibilities will increase. At the moment, however, he goes to the Church. If he is received with warmth and help, he sees it as natural, part of the expected compassion of its members. If he is rejected, he becomes angry and condemns. Either way, the streak of compassion which runs through the Bible is seen to be an integral part of the Church which has built itself upon it.

With our traditional adoration of infallibility, it is not easy for us to accept that there is a weakness in church and Bible which is part of their very nature; but it is a guarantee of life until, if ever, the Body of Christ and the Society of Man become synonymous.

# TWO

## THE CHURCH IN THE WORLD

1

THE SALVATION MACHINE
*by Patrick Watson*

2

WITH LOVE TO THE CHURCH
*by Monica Furlong*

3

THE CHURCH IN A SECULAR AGE
*by John Wilkins*

Patrick Watson is perhaps the Canadian Broadcasting Corporation's most controversial figure. As co-founder and host of "This Hour Has Seven Days," he has helped to create the only regular public affairs program in Canadian television to reach a nation-wide mass audience.

Monica Furlong is a widely-read English journalist who writes for such papers as The Guardian and Punch. Her most recent book, upon which her essay is based, is With Love to the Church.

John Wilkins is a layman in the Church of England and assistant editor of the magazine Frontier, which explores a wide range of social and religious issues and is considered by many to be the best oecumenically-based journal published in English.

# 1   THE SALVATION MACHINE

Some time ago I attended a service at which we had a sermon on the world situation. We were told reassuringly that the Russians, having a Godless government, were sure to go under in the world struggle, and that the Christian West must triumph. I left the church sadly. If the Church of Christ were to move into the electronic age, such a piece of juvenile fantasy would never be spoken again in the pulpit, and possibly, before long, hardly even thought. You couldn't get away with it. The feedback would be overwhelming. Feedback is a prime characteristic of communication in the electronic age, and a community of worshippers truly come of age in its ways of communicating will feed back constantly to its spiritual leader. He will live and work and preach in and from a state of mind that is rich and many sided and always changing. Dynamic, not static; not singular and narrow and unaware.

The really effective communicators of the age have the ear of the community, and vice versa. Across the continent the radio phenomenon called the Hot Line (or Speak Your Mind, or any of a hundred other titles for the broadcast telephone conversations) is peeling back the skull of the community and revealing to the broadcasters the shape and pattern and the writhings of the naked brain beneath.

How well-equipped or willing the broadcasters are to serve (instead of to exploit) what they see revealed there, is another question. But the great, sad, modern ecclesiastical fact is that the Church, which ought to be a daring leader in the service of the new hip world and is strong enough and rich enough to do it; the Church which could operate closely with the best sources of information in the country in any field of human endeavour, still behaves almost as though the *telephone* had not yet been invented, let alone the electron tube.

Pierre Berton, a man whose antennae have proven to be extraordinarily well tuned-in to his audience, is right, and speaks with valid authority and a well-informed conscience when he faults the Church in communications. The preacher cannot preach any more, nor the healer heal, because the Church will not tune itself in; it will not engage with the modern media in a compact for salvation.

Suppose it would. What an irresistible compact that would be! This is a time in history when the nerve-ends of the people are flayed raw with the input of information, and quivering with desire for, among other things, interpretation. Walk down any street and notice the images, the signs, the wonders, the symbols that the great world thrusts at you from all directions. They are brilliant, vivid, seductive, contradictory. The vividness compels us; the contradictions spark a hunger for interpretation. It is efficient, this information universe of ours, and the very efficiency induces anxiety. What if something goes wrong! What if the power goes off! Note, for example, that a rendezvous established by telephone, will be re-confirmed close to the time appointed; if not, the parties will be anxious. A rendezvous established by an older, less efficient technique such as a letter, will not need re-confirmation and much less anxiety will attend the whole arrangement.

So, contemplate the combination: on the one side, an anxious and confused population, its minds buzzing all night with the persistent reverberations of a world that never stops talking to itself; exquisitely sensitive to information input (especially electronic), nervous as hell and ready to jump for any overhanging branch. On the other, a highly organized Salvation Machine, programmed and equipped for electronic involvement. Unbeatable. Terrifying.

But relax.

Only the first half of the combination now exists, its hungers largely unfed.

There are some Salvation Machines operating in the media. Some are effective, if you just look at the outside. The faith healer, Oral Roberts, paralyzes the revival tent and the TV viewer simultaneously, as he magically activates the paralyzed and wins souls for God and Oral. But the Oral tradition is really out of date, after all, in the narrow singularity of its vision and intentions and the simple credibility of its magic. Let us leave that behind; there are complex and unbelievable magics to be done in the world.

They will involve not telling and showing, but knowing and conversing.

But we are not ready. The fundamental weapons are missing from the arsenal: techniques and equipment for transmitting *and receiving*; we lack a modern idiom. Where do we get these weapons, and exactly what is it we need?

Let's start with attitudes. As long as the priest believes that his job is to tell the good news and perform the sacraments and that ordination prepares him for the job, everything is lost. There has to be a fundamental change of attitude towards knowing and the known. The conventional wisdom of the priesthood is that the priest knows, and the people do not know, and they must be told. Perhaps the opposite is true. Almost any priest who claims to know his people is probably out of his skull, instead of into theirs, as he should be. David Clarke, a good and wise priest, once said to me and his other parishioners à propos relations with the largely Jewish population of his parish, "How can we show them we love them if we don't even know who they are?"

It's not enough to know the Word of *God*; the Word of God is meaningless to the priest who does not know the words of man; and the words of man are changing at such a rate that we all have to run to keep up. That priest will save souls who decides at the outset that he has more to learn from the people than they have to learn from him; and then doesn't rest until he has discreetly and thoughtfully lifted off the tops of a great many skulls, contemplated what he finds there, and gently re-covered them. Like all cranial surgery this will be a delicate and dangerous business. He will in many cases find things he would wish not to know about. But know he must if he is to converse; converse he must if he is to convert. How to begin? What are the rules?

IT IS MORE BLESSED TO RECEIVE THAN TO TRANSMIT / Assuming at least the beginnings of a receptive attitude (twitching antennae, and eye prepared to rove the dial), I see the young priest readying himself by repeating over and over again, "*The act of observation alters the observed.*" Now this is not always as true in human relationships as it is in electron physics, say, where the operation of observing the position of an electron causes the electron to change its position. But those who are professionally engaged in trying to find out what people think and feel have, for a long time, recognized the importance of being invisible. In some fields of research (pharmaceutical, for example) testing is put into the hands of investigators who don't even know what results are hoped for (which pill is the phony, which group the control). Thus the risk of wishful observation of that which did not in fact occur is reduced to a minimum. We television journalists are continually trying to devise better ways of diminishing the overtness of our operation, so that the camera may observe without causing movement among the electrons whose position it is observing. Our young priest will not aspire to such a degree of sophistication at his listening post, and should not, for he, unlike the scientist, must be one who engages with his world, as well as observing it.

But no observer is less invisible than the clergyman, clad in his usual alienating costume and air of bonhomie and sanctity. You can't help noticing who it is you're talking to, and altering the modes accordingly. The sensors and the censors both operate full tilt on details that ought to be irrelevant. It should be possible for us electrons if this is our normal manner of expression, to say Bullshit! to the priest, without altering anyone's position. But just try it!

Dr. Eric Berne in his admirable book *Games People Play* reminded us that human relations improve when people stop playing games and speak what's on their minds, even when the content is unpleasant. But conversation with the minister is characterized by an excess of concealment of real feeling and normal ways of speaking.

In that radio hot line I mentioned above, people say what's on their minds for hours to broadcasters all over the land. But what kind of people are they, you ask, who'll display so much of themselves in public, who talk such banal nonsense, such spewings of second-hand views unencumbered by thought or discipline? What sort of person would waste his time on *that* sort of thing! Well, brother (or sister, or Father), if you do say anything faintly resembling the above, you're not with it. You're out of it, man. Your antennae have gone limp. Because these are exactly the kind of people who, all around you, speak a language you don't understand, that you need to understand, a spreading, nervous, vital language. These are the people you've lost and need back; the truly modern men who need you almost as terribly as you need them, but who, because they haven't got you, turn to the real participation of the hot line, or the imagined participation of the TV show. How many clergymen would find it not beneath their dignity to place a few calls, regularly – in civvies, so to speak – to some of these programs, to give the benefit of their ordained wisdom to the thousands who are not just listening, but communicating? It might be a rude experience, but it's virtually a virgin field, and an arena where thousands of people nightly display their hunger for contact and interpretation and their astonishing grasp of the way the world works – for them.

What might happen?

| | |
|---|---|
| *The Rev. V. Eager* | Good evening. |
| *The Hotliner* | Yeah? |
| *The Rev.* | Ah, well, I've been listening to this talk to-night about how tough the divorce laws are, and I'm struck by the fact that no one seems to pay the least attention to the idea that marriage is a sacrament, and that God has acted in it, and it's not up to man to tamper with it. |
| *Hotliner* | I see, Sir. Would you say that you are a religious fanatic? |
| *The Rev.* | No! No, no, no; I'm not a fanatic at all, but I . . . |
| *A.N. Other Caller* | (Later) I was listening to that guy a while back and I think he's some kind of a nut. I mean people get married to have sex, or maybe they had it and got caught you know. Ha ha. Or maybe they even *want* to have kids. But what's all this stuff about sacraments? I mean that just isn't in it. |
| *Hotliner* | Oh well, I don't know. That gentleman is entitled to his opinion just as much as you are, you know. How do you know there's nothing in what he says? |

Could that lead to something useful? Could churches buy time for hot lines of their own? If they could, is there anyone around who could conduct such an affair with the necessary candor and humour and interest in the extraordinary qualities of ordinary people?

Now all this about the hot line is just a hazarded notion, not a prescription. I don't mean to suggest that the way to get with the electronic age is to get involved in broadcasting. There's a certain amount of evidence that the quickest way for a church to *lose* touch with the people is to put on a television show. While the clergy are busy deploring the dearth of quality in religious programs on television, the viewers aren't the least bit busy deploring the deathly quality of the religious programs that do get on; they simply look elsewhere or switch off. The professional broadcasters ignore the world of religion most of the time because, in their terms, it's dull. Sometimes a guitar-playing nun makes the "Ed Sullivan Show," or a dissenter catches the attention of "This Hour Has Seven Days," and this is good, but not good enough to build a Salvation Machine. For the most part, the doings and thinkings and sayings of the men of the cloth are not very interesting to the world of broadcasting. They simply do not seem to take place in the contemporary world.

Why is it that gospellers like the Beatles, who offer, you may think, nothing but more cliches about sex, can, with their brothers of the beat, win the prayers of most of one generation and generous portions of a couple of others? It's not because they have any special vision of the Truth, but because what truth or illusion they do purvey speaks to a world they dig, a world that feeds back to them unreservedly and uninhibitedly, and because they respond to that feedback, playing up what's big this week, playing it down if it doesn't swing next week.

At this point I begin to offend even myself with the suggestion that the bearers of the Word of God should prostitute themselves and bend to every vagrant breeze of popular whim in order to win the favours of the mob. But this just proves that I still bear the scars of my puritan past; that the electronic age moves too fast for the emotional flexibility of even its ordained ministry. In fact, there is no suggestion here of prostitution, no heretical proposal that the Truth be decided by democratic vote. All I am saying, and I insist on it, is that the *forms of transmission* must be conscious of fashion and swing with the times. It may even be necessary to scurry and rush to keep up, and if this seems undignified, then I suggest we need a new concept of dignity, for the true dignity may, after all, be found while washing the feet of the people. I find little comfort in such phenomena as this man's jazz liturgy or that man's beat gospellers or the other man's beer missions. Or even in Miss Mollie Batten's marvellous seminal work in Britain in applying the spirit of Christianity to the world as it is and not as it should be. These are isolated individuals; they don't reflect an interest by the institutional Church in the modern world and its ways. The hierarchies of the Church should be rushing to apply every lesson in communication these folk are learning; but the hierarchies of the Church don't rush. Secure in the tremendous and comfortable error that the world will wait for them, they weigh and sift with care, instead of daring and hazarding. While they are busy balancing out this scale and that, the dog will run off with the sausages.

If thou wouldst build a Salvation Machine, this is the fashion which thou shalt make it of. The power plant shall be the same Great Mover as always; safe at the centre of the machine. clothed in its grandeur, speaking of eternity, moving silently and marvellously with its old, wonderful power, its essential fuel mysterious as ever, burning deep and endless. Let there be built around the power plant a sort of engine room where the outside world can be shut out, where words like sanctuary and comfort and rest may find true meaning. Let these things be at the heart, as they always were. But from there on out, let it be modern. Let it have a chassis of the lightest, most flexible alloys. Let it be amphibious, airborne, even orbitable. Equip it with the very newest in radar and depth sounders. Style it and trim it to meet the Pepsi Generation and all the generations that follow. Let its operators be trained in the arts of listening to people who appear to have nothing to say. Let them stay loose and be prepared to re-program the machine's computers every week, if need be. Let them plug it in to Viet Nam and Moscow and Watts and Bogalusa and Hollywood and St. Tropez.

The reorientation of the Church's attitude towards communication would require courage of a kind that the Church as Institution has seldom demonstrated. Church people have been daring enough. They have dared the Amazon and the Arctic and even the state of Mississippi, but the institution, or institutions, have always concentrated on the preservation and enlargement of what they have. And now it is time to risk great losses, to hazard the kind of daring a lover needs who would say to his beloved, *I have betrayed you with another, but it is you that I love. Believe me.* If you who would preach and heal and convert would truly learn to do those things in a world that is shrinking to the size of a single community, and increasingly spending its time examining itself; you must send your soldiers into the world with the command: Reverse your roles! Go among the people that they may teach you! Confess your sins to the people that they may forgive and absolve you! For what shall it profit a Church if it saveth its own soul but loseth the whole world. If the Church is the Body of Christ and is builded on a rock and will everlast, then who in the world can better afford to dare? The risks are great; so are the prizes; and the race is already begun. If you do not now start listening to the people for love, there are lots who will do it for money.

### Monica Furlong

## 2   WITH LOVE TO THE CHURCH

At the heart of the Christian's difficulties at the moment lies his relation to the secular world.

What is odd is that Christians rarely define what they mean by the world. Many biblical texts, as well as the Baptism Service in the Book of Common Prayer, suggest that it is something pretty disreputable that we should do well to avoid, but they never make it entirely clear what it is. The more puritanical writers and thinkers have chosen to identify the world with sexual emotion, and with the colour and gaiety and spontaneity and enjoyment which spring from the senses. They set out to claim that the world is lust and selfishness and greed, which is not necessarily a bad definition; but they actually seem to be saying something else –

that it is pretty girls, virile young men, the act of love, the joy of intercourse, the pleasure of eating, drinking, behaving with lack of inhibition. And if Christians are rejecting this, then they are running curiously counter to the world as God has made it, and to men and women as he has made them.

Or one might define the world rather differently, somewhat as Christ himself seems to have defined it. Christ often spoke of "this world" or "this life," suggesting that it was those who could only see things in terms of "this life" who lost their way and denied truth. If you thought only of "this life," he seems to say, then you could not see that there was anything more important than comfort, wealth, sensual gratification, power, fame, and gradually you came to live for one or another of these things. This was to build your house upon sand, since eventually you discovered that pursued as ends in themselves, these things were no good and only made you more alone and more unhappy.

The meaning and beauty of life came from acknowledging another dimension, another range of thinking and feeling, the range of love, of forgiveness, of self-knowledge, and the knowledge of others. It was only through plunging into this other dimension that men could overcome their isolation and reach one another. It was only because of it that "the world" had any reality at all.

The hopeful thing about some of the most enlightened post-war Christian thinking is that it has begun to hammer out a new way of regarding "this world." In the words of one young theologian I know, "We used, with sublime arrogance, to talk of 'taking Christ to Africa or to China, just as if Christ was not already there.' " Christ was already in China or Africa long before a single missionary set foot there. Christ was part of the structure of other faiths, of other cultures, of art, of family and social life, of the individual's thinking and feeling. The Gospel, the "good news," consisted in encouraging men to make a discovery: that the instinct within them which they had known all their lives and which had been continually frustrated – the impulse towards vulnerability, towards love, towards freedom – was a true instinct, an instinct which originated in the principle of life itself. Again and again, the European Christian exaggerated the alien quality of the more primitive people to whom he preached Christianity, perhaps in an unconscious attempt at self-protection against the impact of a primitive society upon himself. While he talked of reconciliation, of men being brothers, he etched the dividing lines more and more deeply. The black man might become a Christian but at a terrible price. The price he must pay was to be isolated from his pagan culture and to become an imitation white man.

Now if the Christian cannot deny what he believes to be the truth, he can be infinitely more humble in his approaches to others. It seems to me wrong for him to adopt a fiercely militant approach to the unbeliever, wrong for him to play upon others' sense of guilt, wrong for him to talk of "strategy" as if conversion were a sales campaign or a political manoeuvre. It is wrong because it shows no reverence for the personality of the unbeliever, no acknowledgement that he may have reasons – intellectual or psychological – which would make it either dishonest or dangerous for him to accept belief at that particular time. It is not enough to think that since Christianity is truth, then it does not matter how clumsily it is rammed into people. If it is truth, then it must be sought always upon the far side of others' integrity. We must trust the reality of faith enough to believe that if we encourage others in a fearless search for truth and do not worry where it leads them, it will in the end lead to Christ.

For many, of course, the search is not primarily an intellectual search, but a search for a healing of the personality and its wounds. The man who rejects God because he identifies him with the father who rejected him, the woman who is locked in neurotic anxiety or depression, is not principally concerned in discovering a faith but in finding healing for nagging emotional wounds. If we think that the answer for such people is to be pressed immediately into the Christian camp, we may do more harm than good. All that we may be able to do for other people is to care about their suffering and ease it if we can; to tell them the truth, to encourage them to live in the real world rather than in a fantasy one. But then this *is* a step toward Christ, in many cases a more appropriate one than churchgoing. We may only be able to offer Christ to the agnostic through our love and honesty, not through the doctrine, the sacraments or the fellowship of the Church.

If, however, the Christian challenge to the agnostic is to be the greatest of which he is capable, the greatest self-knowledge, the most valiant attempts to live in reality instead of in fantasy, then the Christian himself needs to change out of recognition. The Church has encouraged us to believe that what is chiefly needed for spiritual health is the routine of prayer and the liturgy, of confession and the sacraments. These things are, of course, infinitely precious, a life-giving and sanity-preserving framework of life and more besides: the foretaste of the abundant living talked about in the gospels. Yet the disturbing fact remains that too many who faithfully practise these things do not seem liberated people. In many cases, the faith which should have led to enlightenment and self-knowledge has become a means of evading reality, of retiring into a fantasy world which is safer and nicer than the real one. Within fantasies such as these, men do not have to grow, nor to grow up, do not have to pay the terrible price of maturity, which is to bear the knowledge of their fears and their desires.

Until a few years ago, it seemed unbelievable that tuberculosis or typhoid or diphtheria could be controlled, but the upsurge of confidence and belief in medical advance made such a victory possible. What is needed now is a new understanding of love, the love that casts out fears and enables men to face the realities of their condition. As there is a hygiene of the body which, properly carried out, strengthens its resistance to disease, so there is a hygiene of the mind and of the spirit. We know more and more about the emotional environment that a child needs in order to grow up fearless and outgoing, able to give love and receive it. To my surprise, the Church talks little about these requirements, but far too much and far too critically about the adolescents and adults whose lives have already been irreparably damaged by emotional impoverishment.

To learn this hygiene, however, is a task which will take several generations. In the meantime, we all have to recognize our own emotional inadequacies and the way these interact upon our children and our friends. Failure to do so means that we are seriously handicapped in offering the love which we claim to be the Christian contribution to society.

Some of the loneliest people in our community are those who have failed in one way or another in the ideal code of behaviour we have laid down: the unmarried mother, the young man who has discovered that he is homosexual, the divorcee, the man or woman who is haunted by thoughts of suicide and may have made more than one attempt at it, the middle-aged man who has committed adultery. Would any of these people turn automatically to the local Christian community, in the confident expectation that they would receive love and understanding?

Some of these people might, and do, turn to a parish priest for comfort and help, or to some special Christian organization specifically designed to help them. But if the priest is to solve their loneliness permanently, and is to offer something more valuable than a clinging and dependent relationship upon himself, then he needs an accepting community into which he can introduce those who suffer acutely from a sense of exclusion.

A few churches have such a nucleus of people, but the majority of church-folk are not like that, partly because of an ignorance and a lack of imagination which over-simplifies moral behaviour, partly because they fear that to forgive anti-social attitudes is to condone them. This is the old fear: that truth will not prevail, that the moral structure of a nation is so fragile that it needs elaborate defences. Christians, it seems to me, have to choose between the safety of "morals" and the danger of love. It is my own belief that Christ's teaching was principally about the latter, but that if you do teach men and women to love God and love their neighbour then morals take care of themselves.

Love must be a process of learning to be vulnerable – to one another, to ideas, to knowledge, to the arts, even to the injuries which the forces of evil constantly try to inflict. It is impossible to love without getting hurt, if only because the loveless may be incapable of responding to love. The Christian must love "this world," not in a desperate attempt to be "with it," but for its own sake. It is beautiful enough if we do not perpetually sour it with condemnation. The purpose of the Christian revelation was not that we should end up like Bertrand Russell, claiming that "life is horrible, horrible, horrible." The Christian has discovered meaning and joy on the far side of waste and agony; he has experienced the Resurrection.

As for our fear that the Christian sands are running out, that not only Christian morals, but Christian beliefs and practices as we know them, are in imminent danger of being swept away on the tide of secularism; I believe that we must learn to face with equanimity, even with enthusiasm, the prospect that it might happen, working out for ourselves in the process the kind of faith which could survive and make sense to us, even in the most hostile conditions.

It was no accident that it was Bonhoeffer who explored the relevance of Christianity to a godless society. Deprived of his freedom and the right to work as a pastor, separated from friends and fellow-believers, confronted daily by brutality and himself the victim of it, it was not surprising that for him the old answers, even the old questions, made no sense. For the Christian in such circumstances the questions become very simple. What did Christ's death on the cross mean? Did He really triumph over evil or did evil triumph over Him? Was there, *is* there a Resurrection? Is it true that if we commit ourselves to love the gates of hell shall not prevail against us? Or is the life of man a futile, meaningless, painful struggle in which the ruthless and the violent usually win?

The pain of the Christian vocation can be such that we do not often feel like asking these questions, and would much rather retreat into administration, respectability, good works, elaborate piety, or stern morality. But our contemporaries quite properly expect answers and are contemptuous of our attempts at escape. If we have lost our revelation about love and meaning, then we are of no use to the world at all. But if we can rediscover it, then we are at one with Christ, at one with the Suffering Servant, in building up the old wastes, raising up the former desolations, repairing the waste cities, the desolations of many generations. Like the Suffering Servant we shall be permitted to bind up the broken-hearted, to proclaim liberty to the captives and the opening of the prison to them that are bound, to proclaim the acceptable year of the Lord.

"And the Gentiles shall see thy righteousness, and all Kings thy glory."

## 3 THE CHURCH IN A SECULAR AGE

It seems to me that in his heart (and he will forgive me if I am wrong), Pierre Berton still loves the Church, and therefore considers that any new thing which arises outside of her is a mark against her. This is a mistake. The world of the New Age is secular. Within it, Christian and non-Christian are engaged in a common enterprise and face together common problems. As the great Roman Catholic theologian Father Congar said during the second Vatican Council, "The human and the Christian are coinciding more and more. It is no longer possible to separate anything from anything." A world come of age in this way rightly demands freedom from ecclesiastical control.

But "the Church" is not equivalent to "the clergy"; over ninety-nine per cent of her members are laymen. Mr. Berton's book hardly ever takes account of this. To such an extent have Christians failed to show how every believer shares Christ's priesthood. Freedom from ecclesiastical control does not mean freedom from God's control. The layman must keep before him always the Christian perspectives within which he has to see all the phenomena that confront him, and he must then work out, in his own way, what this means for him in his daily task.

One thing it can mean runs counter to the main drift of Pierre Berton's book. He takes it for granted that Christians should always be leaders in the march of the world's moralists. On the contrary, it can be important to deflate a situation, to take the moralizing out of it and expose the Pharisaism with which we trick out our desires in the clothes of crusading virtue. In the nuclear era, we have good reason to be apprehensive of nations or individuals who discover in themselves a messianic vocation. Christ sometimes spoke of his followers as leaven, working within society a hidden transformation.

But He spoke of them also as lights which were not to be hidden. I think that the Christian missionary movement is one of the most remarkable episodes in history, and I still think so in spite of Pierre Berton's assessment of it. He writes:

*Imperialism . . . begins with the missionary. If the missionary is unconscious of the fact that he is an advance scout for the political invader (as he certainly has been), this does not meliorate his error.*

But you cannot make a fool of Jesus Christ as easily as that. Let us take in contrast a remarkable tribute from Ndabaningi Sithole, a Rhodesian political detainee:

*. . . When Europeans took our country we fought them with our spears, but they defeated us because they had better weapons. So colonial power was set up much against our wish. But lo! the missionary came in time and laid explosives under colonialism. The Bible is now doing what we could not do with our spears. . . .*

Sithole goes on to say that in parts, at least, of Africa, the Church has created a Christian consciousness which transcends the normal barriers of race and colour and thus gives a "creative purpose and direction to African nationalist consciousness." He points out that almost all important African political leaders went through the Christian Church school.

After Constantine, the Church was committed to the experiment of working out an organic relation between Church and State. The result was the remarkable phenomenon of Western Christendom. But the cost to the Church has been heavy, and the structures which were built up are now in process of dissolution. Pierre Berton calls the second section of his book, "The Tyranny of the Religious Establishment," and someone who belongs, as I do, to an established Church, knows only too well what he means. The class ladder of the Protestant and Anglican Churches, from Episcopalians down to – or is it up to? – Holiness sects; the frustration of oecumenism as much by these class differences as by doctrinal differences; the right-wing drift in politics endorsed, at least till recently, by all the major churches from Geneva to Rome; irrelevant sermons and "dead" services; the rigidity and bureaucracy of an outdated parochial system, geared to a vanished rural economy; the proliferation of ecclesiastical "plant" where it is not needed, at the expense of the areas which need it most – all these things are only too evident.

The establishment problem is a real problem, and there is probably no ideal solution. Let the words spoken in 1846 by Thomas Chalmers, that arch-opponent of establishment, be a warning to us of the kind of attitude which a policy of complete separation can lead to:

*We leave to others the passions and problems of this world, and nothing will ever be taught, I trust, in any of our Halls, which shall have the remotest tendency to disturb the existing order of things, or to confound the ranks and distinctions which now obtain in Society.*

Chalmers had left the Established Church of Scotland in 1843, together with a considerable number of followers, to found the Free Church of Scotland.

There are signs everywhere of a ferment of thinking in the churches about all this. The acceptance of sociological techniques as relevant to enquiries into the structure of congregations is one such sign. Another is a changed theory of ecclesiastical authority, drawing its analogies now, not from military or industrial chains of command nor from the procedures of the law court, but from the community of the family. We are experimenting in new forms of ministry, worker-priests or priest-workers, and we are trying out more mobile forms of church life, like "house churches." We are thinking about how a "parish" can now be based on coherent areas of community life, such as docks or shopping centres, rather than on geographical areas as such.

At the start of the Church's history it was said, "See how these Christians love one another." The unity of the Church is the context within which such a saying makes sense, and must be restored if it is to be said again. Let the Church be the Church, as Pierre Berton asks. Whatever helps to build up a community whose members truly love each other because they live in Christ – in the truth – must be retained. Everything else, if necessary, can be scrapped. Again as Berton writes: ". . . The participation of the congregation in the Communion Service perhaps, after all, is the only real and vital need of a true Christian."

Pierre Berton draws heavily on John Robinson, and I share his fascination for the bishop's writing. It gets through to people in a vital way. It may well be that in the present state of our under-standing this kind of theology is the only kind that can get through. Nevertheless, the trend that it represents, if it is thought to be sufficient in itself, is one that proves disastrous. Dr. Robinson starts from where people are. He accepts their unbelief and their preconceptions, and he argues from there. That is his strength. But he accepts too many of their preconceptions. In particular, he accepts that there is an unbridgeable gulf between the world within man and the world outside him. A fear of the cosmos that is almost a neurosis pervades *Honest to God*. The universe is seen as basically hostile. There is a depth in persons, but there is not a depth in things. Confidence is lost that there is any real meaning in the doctrine that Christ was at work in the creation of the world. In the end this is bound to prove fatal. It is not enough just to make statements like Tillich's: "he who knows about depth knows about God." If there is no "without," there can be no "within." Christianity becomes schizophrenic, suffering from an intolerable split between the world within the soul and the visible world without. True, this is the world we know, and that is why Dr. Robinson's theology comes over with such an impact.

Yet it is the artists rather than the theologians who are really describing what it means to be alive today; and what we find in the novels of Sartre or the films of Antonioni or the plays of Beckett is man's alienation and *ennui* in the face of the absurdity and enmity, the hopeless plurality, of the world in which he is set.

If this is the problem with which the deepest imagination of the age is obsessed, theology cannot by-pass it. While the prob-lem is unsolved, we suffer from the atomization of society into isolated units which have trouble understanding each other and often do not see why they should try. No mere improvement in the techniques which the Church uses to communicate is going to be of any use here.

We need again a theology of the whole of things, and this must include a theology of space and time. Pre-Copernican theology had a scheme of the universe which made sense to the men of those days. After Copernicus, theology, by abdicating from the realm of space, evaded the problem he set it. How far is Dr. Robinson's attack on the whole idea of a God "out there" an attempt to continue the evasion?

Such an evasion, if this is what it is, will not fool the layman for long. It is to the layman that theology has to speak now. Working in a factory, in his lab, or at his desk, he bends nature to his will and shapes it for the use of man. Looking in his newspaper at photographs of the surface of Mars, he may even dream of conquering the realms of space. A theology that confines itself to personal relations will influence a part, and the most important part, of modern man's life, but it will not direct his dream.

Meanwhile, there is nothing more important than the training of the laity so that the priesthood of all believers can become a reality. The liturgical movement which groups the laymen round the priest and brings the altar into the centre is a symbol of something which must happen at the level of everyday living. The layman needs much more guidance on how to see all his work as worship and all his life as prayer. Suppose Britain was under communist control, or Canada. Would the faith be carried on by the laymen, as it has been in so many places in Russia, without them feeling that they were being asked to do something very unusual? Pierre Berton quotes John Lawrence, editor of *Frontier*: "For too long in the West the higher reaches of religion were considered a special preserve of the clergy." The Anglican Church must come under severe judgement at this point. She has not taken seriously the need to instruct her laymen, not only in the faith itself, but in the things which follow from the faith, such as a social theory and a social policy. She has not guarded them against the incorrect interpretation of the "autonomy of the secular" (an autonomy perfectly valid in itself), which wrongly considers that the various functions of society – political, economic, legal and so on – are bound so exclusively by their own particular laws and techniques that the Church can have nothing to say within these spheres. This misconception is widespread, and it is a form of polytheism.

What then of the future? Pierre Berton looks for a prophet, and prophets will arise. Some have already come among us. Teilhard de Chardin, for example, is one of them. But we do not have to wait for the future before a revolution can begin. Contrary to what Pierre Berton says, the "one man" who "turns everything inside out" is *not* "unborn." He is the same yesterday, today, and forever.

**THREE**

# DOGMA: WHO NEEDS IT?

**I**

RELIGION WITHOUT DOGMA
*by John A. T. Robinson*

**2**

FAITH WITH DOGMA
*by James A. Pike*

**3**

THE CATHOLIC TRADITION
*by Eugene Fairweather*

*John A. T. Robinson, Bishop of Woolwich and former Dean and Fellow of Clare College, Cambridge, has been known among theologians for such perceptive works as* The Pauline Doctrine of the Body, *and is now known to millions as the author of* Honest to God *and* The New Reformation?

*James A. Pike, Bishop of California, has been involved in many of the new experiments in which the Episcopal Church has been engaged during the past dozen years, and has become a major figure in American public life. He is a trained lawyer, a former atheist, and an ex-Roman Catholic. His latest book is* A Time for Christian Candor.

*Eugene Fairweather, one of North America's leading dogmatic theologians, is Keble Professor of Divinity at Trinity College, University of Toronto. He is the editor of* A Scholastic Miscellany, *the author of several books, an Anglican observer at the Second Vatican Council, and a member of the Committee of Ten for the discussion of Church union.*

**John A. T. Robinson**

# 1 RELIGION WITHOUT DOGMA

When I first read Pierre Berton's book – with the speed which his style and material compels – I replied at once that, of course, I would contribute a chapter to this symposium. He appeared to have encountered enough ecclesiastical equivocation, and I wanted to cheer the courage and imagination of the Anglican Church of Canada in commissioning him. I wanted, too, to add my support to those who were at the receiving end of the panic reaction it provoked – and to reassure them that the fears and insecurities which made it so vehement *do* work themselves out surprisingly quickly; twelve months later one can scarcely believe the old newspaper clippings! But above all I wanted to express my personal gratitude for a book which I found only too uncomfortably near the bone. The comparable book by Paul Ferris on the Church of England (though it was certainly not commissioned) was often perceptive but usually superficial; it was a mirror that showed us our face – warts and all. But Pierre Berton's book got beneath the skin; it was always penetrating and sometimes prophetic.

So I freely agreed to contribute. Only later did I begin to wonder what there was left to say. For he seemed to have said it all so much more succinctly. Moreover, by the time this appears, anything that for the time being I might wish to say about the Church will already have been published in *The New Reformation?*[1] It will be evident how much my book and his quite independently chime in together. Indeed, it is one of the real signs of hope that the same "eve of reformation" feeling seems to be building up all over Christendom in widely separated places. We could well be on the brink of a creative dissolution.

Pierre Berton's chapter "Faith without Dogma" is one in which I took particular interest since it was so sympathetic with what I sought to do in *Honest to God*. By that I do not simply mean that it was kind. One recognized a certain empathy – often so conspicuously missing from the early reviews – in contrast with the early letters.* The difference was well expressed by a student at a public meeting in Scandinavia, who got up after listening to numerous contributions by his elders and said: "These people have understood what you said, but they have not felt what you meant." Pierre Berton, one sensed, was one of those who did feel what it meant.

But what of his own plea for "faith without dogma"? Ten years ago – and, even more, twenty years ago – I should have been very suspicious of such a slogan. My generátion had passed from an undogmatic liberal optimism based on the brotherhood of man and the fatherhood of God, which had shown itself so futile in the face of twentieth century evil, to the need for something much harder. D. R. Davies' *On to Orthodoxy* was a title which rallied many at the time, and in 1940, with the abyss opening at our feet, it was natural to respond to Dorothy L. Sayers' seeming alternative: *Creed or Chaos*. Her earlier pamphlet, *The Greatest Drama Ever Staged*, which ran through six printings in the six months before Munich, opened with the words:

*Official Christianity, of late years, has been having what is known as a "bad press". We are constantly assured that the churches are empty because preachers insist too much upon doctrine – "dull dogma" as people call it. The fact is the precise opposite. It is the neglect of dogma that makes for dullness.*

It did not apparently occur to her that it might be neither, but rather the fact that the dogma as it was preached did not come as the answer to questions anyone was asking.

In any case we reacted. And while the Catholically–minded recalled us to "the Faith once delivered" and Protestants to "the Word of God" (conceived as falling like a plumb-line from heaven), the biblical theologians reminded us that the centre of the Gospel was not the Sermon on the Mount but the apostolic

---

*It is worth reiterating that *The Honest to God Debate* merely reflects the first three months' reactions . Most of the best reviews came later – among them I would single out Albert van den Heuvel's in *The Ecumenical Review*. Historians will get a very distorted picture simply by citing those who were quickest on the draw.

preaching of Jesus, the Son of God, crucified and risen (the so-styled *kerygma* – a word uglier even to the English ear than dogma). "Faith without dogma" in turn came to have a bad press, and still there is a part of me that jibs at any such program.

Part of the trouble is, of course, that the word "dogma" itself is so emotionally loaded. In origin it is as innocent as the very tentative term translated, "it *seemed good* to the Holy Spirit and to us," from which it derives. Dogma was simply what the Church decided or defined as it went along. But, with the hardening of the centuries, it acquired the authoritarian, prescriptive overtones from which it now cannot escape. The definition has become so identified with what it seeks to define, that "faith without dogma" inevitably suggests either "faith without content" or the warm but vacuous "faith in faith" said to beat at the heart of the American Way of Life.

No one, least of all Mr. Berton with his closing vision of a modern Suffering Servant, wants that. All the most astringent, invigorating elements in contemporary Christian renewal (many of them tracing their line through the blood of martyrs to Dietrich Bonhoeffer) envisage a very distinctly Christian style of life, with a temper and a cutting edge of its own. Indeed, everywhere there are signs of a sharpening, a stripping down, a paring away. And *in this context* the summons to faith without dogma takes on a different significance. It is part of the stripping down, of the preparedness of the Church to come out of its shell and live without walls. What it calls in question is not the centre but the circumference – the perimeter with which the Church surrounds itself, whether of creed or code or constitution.

In this sense I would certainly support the call for a flexible and open-ended approach. I applaud the new title chosen for the bulletin of the Youth Department of the World Council of Churches – *Risk*. For our God is a God who moves, who goes on before, who calls us out not knowing whither we go. Our norm is "way out," not safely consolidated behind us. The Church's concept of truth must be an inductive one, implying a genuine exploration. Indeed, it is out of such an understanding of truth that "dogmas" first got formed: they represented the established hypotheses, the agreed results, *to date*. The betrayal occurs when they become the final formulae, the answers at the end of the book to which somehow the sum must be made to work out. The venture of faith is then no longer an open-ended search for the truth. Instead, the truth is settled in advance, and faith is bringing oneself to believe it. If this is what dogma signifies – and, let us face it, in popular language it is – then we must be prepared for faith without dogma.

Obviously, the distinction did not matter so much when most canons of truth and falsehood, right and wrong, were paternalistic. But people today do not understand "given" truths. Yet our whole concept of authority in the Church remains a deductive one. The traditional image of authority indeed is of something lying behind one, looking over one's shoulder, and breathing down one's neck. The very derivation of the word from "author" suggests a going back to the fount and origin. The norms, whether of faith or morals or church order, are conceived as set in advance; thenceforth it is simply a question of working them out. But today any authority which is to have a chance of being compelling (and therefore authoritative) must *authenticate itself* in the search, the faithfulness, the obedience. The truth has to be discovered in the doing ( a very biblical notion) and precisely what it means cannot be known in advance. And in this hazardous but exciting situation the Christian surely more than anyone else should have the confidence to trust the truth, to be open to the future and be free. For his calling is to be *teleios* (Matt. 5:48), to let his life be directed, not from behind, but by the *telos* or goal ahead. But the word "perfect" by which that term is traditionally rendered has come to mean – whether applied to Christ or to the Christian – a static sinlessness from which all the movement and quest (and questioning) has been drained away.

This same attitude of reaching forward must be the characteristic mark not only of the individual Christian, but of the Church as such. As Harvey Cox puts it in his stimulating book *The Secular City*,[2] the Church's job is to be "God's avant-garde," to keep up with the advance of the Kingdom wherever it may have reached. To say that God works, and is to be met with, in history suggests to most Christians something confined to the past. But what it really means is that in all ages the characteristic place where the God of the Bible is to be found is in *social change*. And it is here, "at the perilous moving edges of change,"[3] that the Church too must be found – before anyone else. This is its calling, which never stands still. It is indeed an impossible vocation; for the Kingdom of God is always there in advance, overtaking and anticipating with its presence and its claim any human response.* But the essential point of the Church is nevertheless to be the first-fruits or avant-garde. And this means, among other things, quite simply *to be there* first – one can scarcely help adding, with a certain cynicism, "for once."

For, as Mr. Berton has shown time and again (and that without any unfair digging up of the past), the Church has so constantly been the *last* to get round to where in retrospect one can see God's justice and compassion were beckoning. In the issues where leadership is required – and that means where risk is required – the Church drags its feet and finally comes in when the real battle has moved on. It is the repeated story over war, racial discrimination, capital punishment, contraception, homosexual legislation, and indeed almost everything to do with sex. It is true that on most of these issues Christians have been in the van of reform, but it is also Christian fire to which they have chiefly been exposed. And even when the spoken record of the Church has been reasonably good (as in Britain of late on colour or homosexuality or the death penalty), it never seems to occur to an official Church body that the corollary of this might be massive support for the *agents* of change. When the Church discusses its own affairs it is quick to recognize that decisions must be translated into budgets and quotas. When it debates the concerns of the Kingdom in society at large it appears to reckon its job done if its "voice" is heard. It leaves it to individuals to carry the cost and face the controversy. But if, for instance, when the Church of England had spoken its mind in favour of the Wolfenden Report on homosexuality or the end of hanging, or urged the duty of responsible parenthood or religious freedom, it had voted even a thousand pounds a year to the Homosexual Law Reform Society or the Campaign for the Abolition of Capital Punishment or the Family Planning Association or Amnesty, then the world might have taken it seriously and the politicians might have had some courage pumped into

---

*Cf. Matt. 12:28 and Luke 11:20: "Then be sure the Kingdom of God has already come upon you.

them. As it is, out of its total annual resources of £42,750,000, no less than £40,500,000 is spent by the Church on servicing itself, whether at home or abroad; and half of the remainder goes on maintaining church schools. Similarly, in the United States, in the Episcopal Church, with one of the better records, the expenditure from central funds on all forms of social action per member per year is 15 cents.

With a financial structure like this – quite apart from its organizational structure – the Church cannot by definition be God's avant-garde. The story is bound to be one of too little and too late. And yet it need not be so – as the honourable exception of the Society of Friends shows.

What one would like to see in every denomination is a budget of opportunity deliberately set aside so that the Church could actually take the initiative for once. When a new area of need or action, of reconciliation or reform, presented itself, we could go in and be there *first*, as the servant Church we are meant to be. Then men might be convinced that we were more than a spiritual preservation society. And they might see the sign, which they do not see now, that we could conceivably be the carrier of the new life for the new age.

At the moment the Church is in danger of collapsing under its own weight, obsessively preoccupied with institutional survival, in the belief that it will thus preserve itself. "And," adds Mr. Berton, "of course, it will preserve itself, as a fly is preserved in amber, or a corpse in glacial ice, or a fossil embedded in imperishable granite." But in Britain at any rate, where the outward façade is less successful (and, one is bound to add, the pressure to conform is less terrifyingly potent), the metaphor supplied to him by an "ex-minister" is perhaps disquietingly nearer the truth. The Church, he says, "is very much in danger of dying from bloodletting. Because it doesn't use its blood, because it hasn't got the normal healing qualities that grow out of vigorous activities, it is liable to suffer a wound from which it will slowly bleed to death, and no one will notice its going when it finally expires. It will leave a residue, but its impact will virtually be gone."

I see that all around me as an only too real possibility. And yet I do not despair. I should despair if I thought this process would merely intensify the struggle to keep the roof on and maintain the ministry and "get people in." But I believe there are sufficient signs of a radical minority prepared, if necessary, to let such things go, in the overriding conviction that if the Church is to find its life it must lose it – for others. This does not mean – as I well know as a bishop with heavy responsibilities for keeping the machine going – that one contracts out of responsibility for the structure or the organization of the Church. On the contrary, I am convinced that one must work away from the inside to re-cast the organization, the plant, the theology, the morals, the liturgy, and everything else. It is a formidable program, but, in the Church of England at any rate, it *is* going on "with all deliberate speed." The votes in the Church Assembly, despite the speeches, are generally in the right direction.

But at the same time one has to recognize that *everything* done from this end will be insufficient. No reformist policy that hopes to render the revolution unnecessary has, in my judgement, a chance. Social change (and the challenge of the reign of God that comes through it) is too fast. We shall be caught with our clothes off. The only question is whether our nakedness will then disclose us exposed for death or stripped for service. That depends on whether within the walls – of structure, of organization, and of thought forms – we have advanced sufficiently in learning to live without them. And here the inner strength is far more important than the outer shell. That is why I welcome what before I would have distrusted, the call to the risk of "faith without dogma."

## James A. Pike

## 2    FAITH WITH DOGMA

"I am quite sure," wrote the young Luther, "that the Church will never be reformed, unless we get rid of canon law, scholastic theology, philosophy, and logic as they are studied today, and put something else in their place."[1] Commenting on this statement, the Bishop of Woolwich says; "If pressed about *what* he would put in their place, I suspect he would have been less sure."[2] I suspect that the same comment would be relevant in connection with the section in *The Comfortable Pew* entitled "Faith without Dogma." This suspicion has some grounding in Mr. Berton's text. His critique of the dogmatism of the Church is a sound and convincing one; his plea for a greater degree of demythologization and a larger measure of agnosticism on the part of Churchmen is convincing; and his examples of ecclesiastical resistance to change, in the realms of irrelevance and incredibility, are telling. But as to what it is that we *are* to believe in he gives only these clues: "Faith . . . in Christ, and not in dogma," "Faith in God about whom that dogma speaks." As in the case of a recent work of mine,[3] this is a plea to distinguish the "earthen vessels" from "the treasure";* but I believe that the treasure requires a somewhat fuller statement than these few positive words found in Mr. Berton's chapter. (I am sure he would agree with me, since we are not to assume that his work is intended as a full, positive statement of the Catholic Faith). And I am further convinced that what *is* to be said of the Faith is *dogma*. This may seem to be mainly a quarrel about the meaning of words. If "dogma" means outdated propositional theology, then by all means let's have none of it. But without any substitute words provided, the phrase, "Faith without Dogma" would seem to imply faith in faith. If we provide something of objective reality to follow the phrase "Faith in . . . ," we have a dogma, however it is stated. I am willing not to press the point further, because I, in fact, share Mr. Berton's visceral reaction to the word dogma; and I will turn instead to the constructive task of seeking to state what I am convinced is "the heart of the matter" – faith which distinguishes the Christian from those who are grasped, consciously or unconsciously, by other world-views. Depending upon whether or not we discard the word dogma, the question is this: "Faith *with* what dogma?" "Faith in *what*?"

1    *God* / In and through and under all things is universal Reality, not a being beside other beings, not a person beside other persons

---

*But we have this treasure in earthen vessels, that the excellency of the power may be of God, and not of us.

(and certainly not three of them). He is all that we mean by personal – and more. As such He can relate to persons, and persons to Him. He is equally and fully present at all places and at all times. The fullness of His love, acceptance, and new life is ever and constantly available. He does not make particular decisions in either this situation or that. He does not change His mind. But there is a variation in situations according to the degree to which He existentially is in them, because of the varying degrees of barrier or openness to Him in different lives at different times. He is good and powerful to a degree beyond any human capacity for either goodness or power. Relationship with Him is not only pragmatically wise, but essential to our own true fulfillment.

2 *Man* / Man has been evolved with finiteness and freedom and, within both, there can be the manifestation of God's truth, love, and new life in our lives for our own fulfillment and as a "means of grace" to others. Man displays a perennial tendency to obscure his finiteness to himself and to exercise his freedom in the direction of his supposed self-interest. Too infrequently does he place God first; he tends to give higher priority to various idols which seem more vividly to represent security and success in the light of his various desires and hopes. These idols include not only "worldly" ones, such as are represented by the gods Mammon, Venus, Mars, Apollo, etc., but also "ecclesiastical" ones: the attribution of finality to historically-conditioned creeds, codes, and cults (and they all *are* conditioned by particular times and places). These idols are really what Mr. Berton means by "dogma" – and this form of idolatry can properly be called "dogmatism," whether or not one gives validity to the word "dogma." To be free of all such idols is a prerequisite to full human fulfillment under God. "I am the Lord your God and you shall have no other gods beside Me." Man's responsibility for his life is implied from the fact that there is only one Claimant: "Hear O Israel, the Lord is one Lord. Thou shall love the Lord thy God with thy whole heart, thy whole mind, and thy whole strength."

3 *Jesus Christ* / Here is the fully free man. He freely chose the calling of rabbi and, more than that, the role of Messiah. And he chose, of the many various Hebrew expectations of messiahship,

that of the Suffering Servant. To echo the passage in Philippians 2, He "emptied Himself" – of self-interest and its idols. He did not care what people thought about Him; He assumed the role of a servant; He was obedient to the Claim – and only to the Claim; trusting – and manifesting – eternal life; He feared nothing – even an ignominious death. He was fully "the Man for Others": the channel was fully open so "in Him the fullness of the Deity dwelt bodily" (Col. 2:9) and "God was in Christ reconciling the world to Himself" (II Cor. 5:19). Thus St. Paul in this same passage concludes, "Wherefore God has highly exalted Him"; God's truth, grace and new life fully "came through." This fulfillment is not unique with Jesus Christ; it is everyone's calling. St. Paul's passage begins with the words "Let this mind be in you which was in Christ Jesus, Who . . ." Human beings, in the ages before the time of Christ and after, within the Christian culture and outside it, have to a greater or lesser degree "emptied themselves" and, fulfilled as persons, have served their fellows as men who were not for themselves but for others. And a very high degree of such fulfillment may have occurred unknown to us in remote parts of this world or on other planets around other stars. But in the total fulfillment of this calling, Jesus Christ is unique as far as anything we have known or experienced. He is our Lord and Saviour.

4    *Christian Life* / In our seeking to be whole persons, we are not left alone. We who would follow Him can identify our "downs" with His great Down (as the Jews – and we also if we are true to our common heritage – identify despair and captivity with the Bondage of Egypt); and our "ups" with His great Up (as indeed the Jews can thus identify with the Exodus); continuing in the visible and invisible community of the "saved" and "saving" in remembrance of His Cross and Resurrection; in Word and Sacraments – at one and the same time being and becoming the "Body of Christ" in the world. This is the basis for the courage and love in involving ourselves with the bruised and bleeding around us, showing forth the Cross and Resurrection in what we say and do, "always bearing about in the body the dying of the Lord Jesus that the new life may be made manifest" (II Cor. 4:10) in fellowship with those now committed in this world and those who have passed on who have found this meaning.

All that Mr. Berton said about the non-finality of any formulations applies equally to what is said above. I am not sure that any theologian – or any other individual Christian – would want to say it precisely that way. But I am sure that about this much has to be said in one form or another, if "the treasure" is to be displayed and operative. Whether we wish to call it dogma or not, something like this is the Catholic Faith which represents the completion of the words "Faith in . . . ."

## Eugene Fairweather

### 3   THE CATHOLIC TRADITION

Pierre Berton's plea for "Faith without Dogma" has moved me mightily. It has not persuaded me to give up teaching the subject known as "dogmatic theology," but it has made me reflect on how seldom that subject effectively informs the day-by-day ministry of our clergy, and how badly it must, therefore, have been presented to them in their theological schools.

There is no evading the hard fact of Pierre Berton. He grew up in the Church. He has spent a good deal of time discussing religious issues with Anglican priests. Yet it is painfully clear that he still has only the vaguest notion of what the historic Christian faith is about. In the face of this hard fact I do not see how we can help taking to ourselves the astringent words of a Canadian theologian of another communion: "It has to be recognized that much of the present unpopularity of religious belief is firmly based on the ignorance and incompetence of religious people, and on the theological mismanagement of religious leaders and teachers."[1]

Nineteen centuries of Christian history present us with a quite different conception of faith from the one suggested by Pierre Berton. Faith, as the great tradition of Christendom has known it, is not just a hopeful and generous attitude towards mankind or a judgement that some forms of behaviour are more desirable than others. It is not just the belief that "truth is better than a lie, honesty better than deceit, love and mercy better than hate and mistrust" – a moral ideal expressed in the "general principles laid down by" the Church's founder and "demonstrated by influential Christians across the ages."[2] Certainly Christian belief has urgent moral consequences. But Christian faith sees itself, not as commitment to a human ideal but as response to God's unique self-disclosure in a particular sequence of historical events, culminating in the birth, life, death, and resurrection of Jesus Christ.

This self-disclosure of God, as Christian faith confesses it, is not just the awakening of reverence for "the spirit within ourselves, and in the world around us, which represents ultimate reality."[3] It is the disclosure of the nature and purpose of the Ultimate Reality, transcending man and his world. It embodies a definite viewpoint and teaching about the world and its divine Creator, about man and his destiny, about human history and God's part in it. Of course, it is open to any man to reject this conception. But it is not rightly open to anyone to deny that this is in fact what Christian faith has been about through the centuries.

The individual believer receives God's self-disclosure through the tradition of a community, the Catholic Church, whose very existence is rooted in the history of divine action. The Church's task is to transmit the content of God's self-disclosure, to communicate the life of Jesus Christ through its sacraments, and to nurture its members in the imitation of Jesus Christ.

It follows that the Church must be deeply concerned to keep its witness authentic. It is neither intelligent nor honest to use the word "Christian" as an honorific label for ideas or actions which a particular culture happens to like. The term stands for a response to a definite matter, derived from a particular history. Though there is room for advance in our understanding of God's word, as well as in our obedience to it, the Church's primary duty is to make sure that the content proposed to faith remains essentially the same.

Here is where dogma comes in. Dogma is one means by which the Church seeks to safeguard the distinctive content of the Christian world-view – by upholding the Christian conceptions of God, man, and Christ against rival views.

"The Church," says Pierre Berton, "has moved a considerable distance from the grandiose pretensions of absolute rightness that once allowed it to describe the shape and nature of heaven and the features of the Almighty in specific terms. Now about these areas the Church itself says: 'We cannot know.'"[4] Neither of Berton's extremes, however, describes authentic Christian theology. The mood of genuine Christian faith is neither "We know fully" nor "We cannot know," but "We know in part."[5] No classical theologian can be found who claims more for dogma; the Christian can hardly claim less.

Christians believe that God has really acted and made Himself known in the history of which the Bible speaks. If this conviction is well-founded, then Christian doctrine is possible. In other words, believers can say something meaningful and true about God and his gracious activity in man's history. "We know."

Moreover, Catholic Christians believe that the Church is called and empowered to bear true witness to God's deed and word. If this conviction is also well founded, then Christian dogma is possible, and the Church can rightly claim to define it. "We know."

At the same time, there is an irreducible element of mystery in God's self-disclosure, as Christian faith receives it. "Now we see in a mirror dimly,"[6] said St. Paul, echoed by a long line of Christian teachers. "We are to consider," St. Thomas Aquinas remarked twelve centuries later, "how God is, or rather how He is not."[7] The point is this. Our minds do not apprehend God directly. He makes himself known through the medium of creatures – first, through the very existence of the world which is His creation, and then more fully through the acts and words of His human instruments in history. Since faith depends on God's self-disclosure, no dogma of faith can claim to be exhaustive and therefore altogether definitive. "We know in part."

Dogmas, then, are not meant to be comprehensive descriptions of a divine reality directly apprehended. They are more correctly thought of as "pointers" to the realities of the Christian world-view – to God the Creator and to His "new creation" of mankind through Jesus Christ. As Berton says, echoing St. Thomas Aquinas, faith has ultimately to do with God and Christ, about Whom dogma speaks, and not with dogmas in themselves.[8] The dogmas of God and Christ are not identical with God and Christ; rather, they are images of realities which transcend them.

Yet, as pointers and images, dogmas remain indispensable. The fact that God is not "seen" cuts two ways. Dogmas are inadequate, but we still need them. God is not an object to which we can simply draw attention, nor is His presence in historical events a power that we can observe. God and His action are apprehended in the response of faith to God's word. But dogmas are a necessary part of the Church's witness to that word. As long as "we walk by faith, not by sight,"[9] we shall need doctrinal pointers. As long as our faith can go astray – in other words, as long as it is not sight – these pointers may have to take the definite form of authoritative formulations of the Church's witness. After all, it is not any old "god," but the Creator God of prophets and apostles, whom Christians worship. It is not the "Christ" of anyone's imagination, but the Lord of the apostolic preaching, in whom Christians trust. It is fidelity to this God and this Christ that dogma exists to safeguard.

Of course, as pointers and images, dogmas are open to improvement and restatement. Reflection on the content of dogma may – indeed, ought to – lead to deeper insight. New philosophical perspectives on the world may make it both possible and necessary to translate old dogma into a new conceptual language. But it does not follow that established dogma can ever be simply superseded. The message of Scripture and the dogmas of the Church remain the test of authentic Christian teaching. We may devise statements which probe deeper or speak more intelligibly to our particular culture. But if we mean them to be Christian statements they must point to the God and the Christ of Scripture – not to our own inventions which we arbitrarily choose to call by the same names. That is to say, they must continue to point to the God Whom faith confesses as the independent Creator of a dependent world, and to the Christ Whom faith acknowledges as God's only Son who took our nature upon Him. Because dogmas are imperfect, Christians may endeavour to express their content in new ways. But because dogmas are true, Christians may not presume to replace their content with some new thing.

So far we have been thinking inside the circle of Christian faith. Within that circle – or so it seems to me – the case for dogma is unanswerable. But perhaps Christian faith itself is no longer a live option. Perhaps the Christian world-view, which faith accepts and dogma defends, is unacceptable to intelligent and honest minds.

Whatever may have been the case in the past, perhaps the growth of knowledge has made faith impossible by showing that its assertions are contrary to indubitable truths of experience and reason. If that is really so, then the case for dogma must collapse, because the fundamental claim that faith is a response to divine self-disclosure will no longer be tenable.

Let us get down to cases. If the Christian world-view really includes the odd ideas that Berton seems to identify with Christian dogma, then there is no point in trying to defend dogma. If, for example, the Church has ever expected Christians to accept "the concept of a white-bearded Big Daddy perched on a cloud" or of "the Mysterious Friendly Spirit somewhere 'out there' in space,"[10] it will be hard to take the truth-claims of dogma seriously. If Christian dogma really treats the notion of a "three-layer universe"[11] as integral to Christian faith, or requires us to believe that "some few thousand years ago the world was created in six days,"[12] we shall have to say that whatever dogma may be about it is not about the real world. If Christian faith is concerned with the Virgin Birth, understood just as a "minor question of mechanics"[13] in the story of a great ethical teacher, it may well be dismissed as trivial.

But in reality the historic Christian faith has to do with none of these things – at least as they are presented by Berton.* Faith and dogma are about God the Creator and the dependence of the world on His creative will – not about the shape of the universe or the process of its evolution. Faith and dogma are about God's acts and words in human history, culminating in the story of Jesus Christ – not about odd events in a merely human life.

I suggest that we take a brief look at the classical Christian doctrine of God the Creator. In that doctrine no attempt is made to locate God either in or outside our world, because its framers are firmly convinced that God is everywhere. In traditional theology God's separateness from the world is stated in terms of His independent and unconditioned being, not of His supposed location "up there" or "out there." The great Christian teachers of the past

---

*In fairness to Berton, it must be said that he has frequently been misled by the sweeping and misleading generalizations of J. A. T. Robinson in *Honest to God*.

knew as well as we do that in accounts of God's action "up" and "down" must be symbols which presuppose no particular map of the cosmos. Moreover, even if the primitive Christian imagination did live in a "three-layer universe," the adoption of new cosmologies, under the influence of Greek science,* does not appear to have caused any theological shock in the Church. As for the "six days" of creation, no doubt most ancient and medieval theologians did accept the Genesis story as factual, for want of better information. But if certain later divines, for a variety of reasons, fought hard for biblical literalism against the advance of science, it does not necessarily follow that they were bearing faithful witness to defined Christian dogma. Certainly the fact that at least two great Church Fathers – Gregory of Nyssa in the East and Augustine in the West – felt quite free to interpret the "six days" symbolically shows that they did not recognize the literal interpretation as binding, and no dogmatic definition exists that would make us think differently today.

Berton's indictment of the dogma of God the Creator is evidently not too well founded. I turn last to his treatment of the dogmas concerning Jesus Christ. As it happens, he has very little to say on this question, but between what he does say and what he astonishingly fails to say I think we have good ground for claiming that once again he knows too little to criticize effectively. He seems wholly unaware even of the Church's fundamental doctrine that "in Christ God was reconciling the world to Himself."[14] The Jesus of his argument is purely and simply the great teacher and example. On this supposition the Virgin Birth – the one point of Christological doctrine to which Berton makes any extended reference – must inevitably seem meaningless. The historical and theological question of the Virgin Birth is of course too complex to be dealt with here. But it must at least be said that when theologians affirm the Virgin Birth they see it as a sign of God's "new creation" of mankind in Jesus Christ, not as a mere "ques-

---

*It is a persistent error of many modern writers to suppose that Christians lived happily with a naively "biblical" cosmology until Copernicus and Galileo appeared. In fact, early Christianity moved fairly quickly and easily into peaceful co-existence with Greek cosmological ideas. Thomas S. Kuhn, *The Copernican Revolution* (Modern Library Paperbacks, New York: Random House, 1959), is instructive on this point.

tion of mechanics." By treating it out of context, Berton distorts the specific issue.

I am aware that to dispose of a few misunderstandings of the historic Christian faith is not to prove its truth. In this short essay I have obviously had to present less than the full case for Christian dogma. But I think that I have at least indicated that the popular critics of dogma would be well advised to try again and try harder, because the case they have made against a caricature is altogether too superficial to damage the genuine article.

# FOUR

## OTHER QUARTERS HEARD FROM

1

THE RELEVANCE BIT COMES TO CANADA
*by Peter Berger*

2

THE ROMAN CATHOLIC IN THE PEW
*by Thomas Roberts*

3

A JEW LOOKS AT CHRISTIANITY AND
SECULARIST LIBERALISM
*by Emil Fackenheim*

*Peter Berger is a sociologist at the New School for Social Research in New York. An official invitation to take a critical look at the Church resulted in his book,* The Noise of Solemn Assemblies. *His best known work,* The Precarious Vision, *is an exploration of the culture of our contemporary plural society.*

*Thomas Roberts, a Jesuit who was formerly Archbishop of Bombay, is the author of* Black Popes *and a contributor to* Objections to Roman Catholicism.

*Emil Fackenheim is an ordained rabbi and professor of philosophy at the University of Toronto. His books include* Metaphysics and Historicity *and* Paths to Jewish Belief, *and he has recently contributed an essay to the symposium* Rediscovering Judaism.

# 1 THE RELEVANCE BIT COMES TO CANADA

What unites Pierre Berton with most occupants of the "comfortable pews" he treats so harshly is that for both of them the classical affirmations of the Christian religion have ceased to be plausible. He *and* they would rush to the nearest psychiatrist, if Jesus Christ appeared to them on the road to Damascus. He *and* they are perfectly "comfortable" in the highly secular world-view that is the common frame of reference for most civilized men today. His call to the few holdouts, mostly theologians or other marginal types, to come out and "join the twentieth century" is in line with everything that is happening in contemporary culture. This may be a very reasonable program, but it hardly merits the description "revolution." What would *really* be revolutionary would be to take seriously the beliefs of the New Testament, of the early Christian confessions, or of the sixteenth-century Reformers.

When it comes to the secularized versions of its old contents, it can hardly be argued that the Church is doing such a bad job of communication, especially in North America. The Church is, by and large, solidly in tune with the general culture. It is respected, reasonably well attended and supported, very much part of the overall cultural scenery. Nor does this really trouble Berton. On the contrary, he urges the Church to fit into the scenery more. He would like the Church to become secularized more rapidly and, as it were, efficiently. This is one point where one may criticize Berton on purely factual grounds. There is something odd about reading of the Church's "rejection of twentieth-century media" in the age of religious bestsellers, radio and television preaching, and a church press in Canada (Anglican, United, and Roman Catholic) whose combined circulation is exceeded only by *Weekend Magazine* and *Reader's Digest* – and reading about it in an attractive best-selling paperback, published under a commission from the Department of Religious Education of the Anglican Church of Canada.

As one of the really promising developments in the "revolution" of the Church, Berton mentions the clinical training movement in the United States. This is perfectly logical. If one identifies God with "the ground of everything personal" and argues that one must be faithful to the mentality of the contemporary age in all one's religious thinking, it follows that one's method in religion must be a science of personality. This science (or so it considers itself) already exists. It is modern psychology. In popularizations, especially of the psychoanalytic variety, this body of ideas has already become a widely accepted guide for the self-interpretation of the man-in-the-street. Berton is thus on the right track if he believes that by adopting this language the Church will become more "relevant" to this man-in-the-street. Only he really should not worry on this score. The Church is *already* using the language and the techniques of contemporary psychology. We can be confident that this usage will greatly increase in the future.

Few readers are likely to argue when Berton tells us that all men, including Christians, should be more deeply concerned with the great moral issues of our time. Nor is one likely to disagree with his focus on the issues of international peace and social justice. But all this has really little to do with the existence of the church in the modern world as such. Priests on "freedom rides" are more appealing than priests at Rotary meetings. They make the Church less reprehensible morally. They will not enhance its intellectual plausibility. But this is just where the heart of the problem lies.

The central ambiguity of Berton's argument is clearly expressed in his conclusions. All through the book he has been telling us that "for this New Age we need a new kind of Church!" He finally suggests that this novel creature will be able "to reach the hearts and souls of men" and that, as a result, it may not only survive but "flourish." A little earlier, in a discussion of new avenues for the ministry outside the parish structure, he imagines that "the Church might get a new kind of recruit, and it might get them in large numbers." In other words, Berton is giving the Church a recipe for success. But only a few pages later, in his final message, he lets loose a flow of rhetoric to convince us that the road ahead, the same road that he is recommending, will be the very opposite of a success story. He speaks of "persecution" and "martyrs." He wants the Church to become "the most uncomfortable institution in the community." He is looking forward to the coming of "some spiritual genius," who will accomplish this purpose, a man who will be a "master of contemporary methods of communication" and who is likely to end up "ragged, cast out, abandoned, denied, and finally extinguished." With this inspiring vision of a public-relations expert gone to seed, Pierre Berton concludes his book, holding out cultural success with one hand and crucifixion with the other. This is more than inconsistency. It is nonsense.

There would be little point to such a sharp commentary on Berton's book if it stood by itself. Its lack of originality and its 'timeliness," however, make it representative of a much broader contemporary phenomenon. Berton's little volume may serve as an excellent example of the more fashionable Christian response to the process of secularization. This is the response of embracing it. It is rapidly replacing the older fashion, the neo-orthodox retrenchment behind the bastions of a theological-ecclesiastical fortress. Pierre Berton's "heresy" is well on the way to becoming an oecumenical ideology, at least this side of the Protestant-Catholic divide, though the *aggiornamento* on the other side is beginning to use the same phraseology, to the justified alarm of such sensitive ears as those of Cardinal Ottaviani. The practical measures that go with the "heresy" have become the stock-in-trade of the "renewal" forces on *both* sides of the divide. Worker-priest experiments, dialogue sermons, jazz liturgies, pop-art Jesus figures – one only has to consult the Christmas, 1964 issue of *Time* Magazine to see that these are anything but the lonely visions of about-to-be-crucified heretics.

In an ironic way Pierre Berton's type of thinking is an important symptom of the very condition which he purports to diagnose – and, up to a point, diagnoses correctly. Contemporary man has a new form of consciousness. To this consciousness, the old religious affirmations appear less and less plausible. It becomes ever more difficult to maintain these affirmations as "objective" truth. By and large, religious thought and practice has taken two attitudes in the face of this predicament. One has to violently affirm the old "objectivities," sharply drawing up battle lines against the ideas coming out of the new consciousness of the world. This has been the stance of the various orthodox movements, "neo" or otherwise. Sociologically, it has had to be accompanied by a sectarian self-enclosure within a Christian subculture. But for reasons much too complicated to be discussed here, the brave bell first rung by Karl Barth in his *Letter to the Romans* in 1919 has come to have a hollow sound about it. The sectarian option seems less attractive, even in Rome.

On the other hand, it seems no longer feasible to go back to the sort of gingerly compromising with modernity that characterized pre-Barthian theological liberalism. The "new wave" is a joyous embrace of secularity, to the point where the ideological shock-troopers within the Church are ready to go further in their abandonment of religion than most people outside the Church. Thus the "radical" theologicans may be ready to throw away such classical religious items as the hope for an after-life or the notion that somewhere, "out there," there is a real God. Many unchurched and even explicitly un-Christian people are much more reluctant.

The procedure of secularization is essentially simple. It has been described by some contemporary German sociologists of religion as "subjectivization." The old "objectivity" is abandoned. There is no God "out there." The history of salvation is a series of events within the individual's biography. There was no empty tomb. The Resurrection is an existential or a psychological phenomenon. "Ultimate reality," in other words, is within the subjective consciousness of man himself – presumably "deep down" in it, the depth generally understood today in terms derived from the Freudian anthropology. On the highest level of sophistication this theological self-liquidation is represented by figures such as Tillich and Bultmann. *Honest to God* and *The Comfortable Pew* represent the same thing at the popular level. Norman Vincent Peale, with whose moral positions the "radicals" disagree so fiercely, differs not one iota from the basic ideological procedure that they employ themselves. The secularizing transformation remains the same on all the various levels of sophistication. Theology becomes psychology. Pastoral care becomes psychotherapy. The devotional life becomes an operation of psychological engineering.

In the area of practice the ideology expresses itself through a number of moral engagements. In the extreme case, these moral engagements constitute the *raison d'être* of the Church. But this is self-liquidating in another way. One may begin by admiring

Christians for their political involvements. But then one must also admire all the others, including the Black Muslims and the atheists, who share these involvements. If the political struggles have become the very reason for being a Christian in the first place, this reason will soon lose plausibility the more one involves oneself in these struggles. If secular aims define the mission of the Church in society, the conclusion that the Church is finally unnecessary is inevitable, no matter how noble the secular aims may be.

Pierre Berton and his ideological mentors are correct. Christianity has become difficult to take seriously today. Some of the reasons for this are spurious, such as those that derive from psychological considerations that are pseudo-scientific and superstitious in character. Other reasons are more weighty intellectually. Modern man has discovered his own loneliness in the vastness of the physical universe. He has also discovered the historical relativity of all propositions about the ultimate meaning of his life. The Christian Church stands or falls with one particular set of such propositions. They are either true or false. One should decide the question and not skirt it by translating its terms to mean something entirely different. All religion stands or falls with the fundamental proposition that man is not the only meaning-giving being; that there is indeed something "out there" that corresponds to human meaning and human hope. This quest for a response to man from the universe into which he finds himself thrown may be illusory as well. If one thinks that, one should give it up and come to terms with an existence bereft of gods. The substitution of the "spirit within ourselves" for the "daddy on the cloud" simply avoids the decision of whether the quest should go on or not. What is more, there is something repelling about the insinuation that those who hope and believe man is not alone in the universe are guilty of psychological malfeasance. It is this, coupled with the fuzziness of argumentation, that in the end leaves a bad taste in the mouth as one finishes Berton's book. One feels like saying about it, and about the broader ideology that it represents, what an Austrian writer said some years ago about psychoanalysis. It is an illness that conceives of itself as its own cure.

## 2    THE ROMAN CATHOLIC IN THE PEW

I am honoured and pleased by the invitation to share in a book inspired by Pierre Berton's critical look at the Church in the New Age. The idea fits well into the ancient Catholic pattern, for the scholastic system on which the training of our priests is based starts with the objections that have become, so to speak, the scaffolding round Catholic doctrine. The danger, of course, lies in the temptation to set up Aunt Sallies of one's own, to demolish them triumphantly, and to glory in our cleverness. That temptation has not been very successfully resisted hitherto.

*During the last few years, there has been much talk about the need for the Church to "listen." We have shown a great talent for lecturing and hectoring; but seem unwilling to believe that God works through men outside our ranks, who may have much to teach us and a few legitimate challenges to make.*

Pierre Berton obviously agrees with this quotation from the foreword to his book by Rev. Ernest Harrison. It is no disparagement of the book to say that the author does not tell us much about the extent and depth of reform already in hand. This is not what he was asked to do. He *was* requested to be completely frank in his criticisms. So he has been, even to the extent of considering the possibility that the Church might cease to function within the next century. He does not wish this to happen, but thinks that it will, if there is no radical change. Mr. Harrison's opinion is "that it will not happen, because there are other roots not dealt with here, and – more important – because I believe that the radical reformation has already begun, and that this book may be one of its symptoms."

A word may be in season as to the sense in which a Roman Catholic could accept the phrase about the Church "ceasing to function." In the nautical language accepted in the phrase "Peter's barque," we would certainly admit that the ship is not only designed by God but that she is guaranteed not to sink and disappear. History demonstrates beyond doubt that she is liable to every hazard of storm, of fog, of stupidity and perversity in the crew, from the captain downwards. She has taken, and may have to take again, batterings so tremendous that she will hardly be recognized as a seaworthy ship, and certainly not as a comfortable ship. Time and time again she has been put into dry-dock, where furious disputes have arisen as to what, if anything, she needed to bring her within the Designer's plan.

Let us take a few examples drawn from the Second Vatican Council, the brain-child of Pope John. First, be it noted that the Council is as nearly oecumenical, or universal in the full sense, as present divisions allow. Not only were some twenty-five hundred Catholic Bishops summoned to it from all nations, but invitations were sent to "observers," both Orthodox and Protestant.

The description marks the difference between the full participator, who speaks and votes, and the observer who does not. The word is accurate, but inadequate; for in fact these brethren *do* participate, both actively and passively. Passively, because their mere presence ensures an attitude of respect, excluding such misrepresentation as was, until recently, common on both sides. Actively, because they are closely linked, both individually and collectively, to Conciliar acts through the commission of unity. Through this Committee, comments and representations may be taken straight to the Pope.

These observers have a voice on many issues in the World Council of Churches. Probably the main stimulus to progress in this Council has been the shock to non-Christians and to half-Christians at the numberless divisions of Christianity. Here again, the observers at the Vatican Council have been invaluable. Their very presence ensures discussion at the deepest level about the kind and extent of co-operation desirable between Roman Catholics and others. Even a cursory reading of the weekly religious press reveals a healthy tension, frightening to those who do not realize that the ship is designed for tremendous stresses from winds, even gales, of change.

In this jet age, thought is apt to move as fast as the plane. We hardly notice how much ground has been covered. Who could have believed, a few years ago, that a deeply respected Cardinal would say, in quasi-public session, that the proceedings of the

Holy Office (late Inquisition) were "a scandal to Catholics and non-Catholics alike"? Who would have thought it possible for an American Cardinal to preach in Protestant churches? Or that, by authority of yet another American Cardinal, an Episcopalian would marry a Roman Catholic in one of our churches, witnessed by ministers of the two religions, and using an Anglican formulary?

Again, while Mr. Berton is no more than just in his severe criticism of Christian failures, both Catholic and Protestant, in the area of social relations and racial rights, we could happily quote notable improvements, both in theory and practice, such as he praises himself.

Of great popular interest is the attitude of Catholic authorities to contraception. Mr. Berton is perhaps inclined to blame too much, and without enough qualification, religious condemnations of birth control. He has suffered himself from ignorant and foolish criticism; perhaps he does not allow sufficiently for the historical fact, undeniable but too easily overlooked, that underpopulation was until quite recently the same kind of threat that overpopulation is to-day. How, in a small Indian town of the thousand souls in the last century, liable to lose hundreds through infant mortality, through under-nourishment, through disease, through lack of all medical and nursing help – how could parents *not* regard fecundity as the chief bulwark of survival? Substantially, that was the picture all over the world. There was not, and there could not be, any substantial difference in the attitude of parents or of civil or religious authorities, Christian or non-Christian. This is a matter very relevant to the Catholic theologian concerned with tracing back a tradition throughout Christian history. How can it be possible to prove a tradition against a practice which could not possibly come up as an issue?

Yet it is beyond dispute that there are many changes in the thinking of religious people, both Catholic and Protestant. Nothing that I can say either in praise of Pierre Berton's criticism, or by way of qualification, is as effective as a speech made by Patriarch Maximos Saigh IV, spoken at the Vatican Council on October 29, 1964. Here was made an authoritative endorsement of Mr. Berton's plea for open criticism, and here too the perfect answer to his challenge. Let it be recalled that the language of the speech, so like that of Mr. Berton himself, came from the lips of a man of about eighty-seven; that he said what would have been unthinkable even perhaps a year ago, and that the Pope has made him a Cardinal.

Said the Patriarch:

*Among the anguishing and sorrowful problems which agitate humanity today, there emerges the problem of birth regulation, a problem most urgent since it is at the bottom of a crisis of the Catholic conscience. There is here a conflict between the official doctrine of the Church and the contrary practice of the vast majority of Christian families . . . On the social plane, the demographic growth in certain countries prevents under the present circumstances any improvement in the standard of living and condemns hundreds of millions of human beings to a shameless and hopeless misery. The Council must give it a valid solution. It is its pastoral duty. It must say whether God really wants this depressing and anti-natural blind alley. — Frankly, should not the official position of the Church regarding this matter be revised in the light of modern science, theological as well as medical, psychological, and sociological?*

*In marriage, the development of the person and his integration in the creating plan of God forms a whole. The purpose of marriage, therefore, must not be dissected into primary and secondary purposes. This consideration opens up a horizon on new perspectives regarding the morality of conjugal behaviour as a whole. And then, do we not have the right to ask ourselves whether certain official positions are not subordinated to obsolete conceptions and possibly even to the psychosis of bachelors who are strangers to this sector of life?*

After closely analyzing some important theological problems and the relief which many felt when the Pope announced that the subject would be studied by the Council, the Patriarch continued:

*In view of the extent and gravity of this problem, which concerns the whole world, we ask that the study should be conducted by theologians, doctors, psychologists and sociologists, in order*

*to find the normal solution which imposes itself. The collabora-*
*tion of exemplary married people also seems necessary. In addi-*
*tion, is it not in line with the ecumenism of this Council to start*
*a dialogue on this matter with the other Christian Churches and*
*even with thinkers of other religions?*

*Why remain closed within ourselves? Do we not have before*
*us a problem common to all mankind? Must not the Church open*
*herself to both the Christian and non-Christian world?*

Be it noted that the Patriarch is spokesman for an increasing number of Bishops from many countries.

Mr. Berton's chapter on war is very fascinating to one engaged, as I was, in three sessions of the Vatican Council and in conversations with Bishops of many nations. I had studied a very strong condemnation by the French Bishops in 1950 of nuclear weapons and of all warfare open to the same objection of indiscriminate killing. I considered with many Bishops the desirability or feasibility of Conciliar statements in the same sense. But we had to face the history of fourteen years since that French condemnation. De Gaulle, supposed to be a sincere and practising Catholic, insisted on admission to the nuclear club. The French people, just as much concerned with "defence" as the rest of the world, showed nothing remotely approaching national revulsion. Neither, on the whole, did the British; the Americans far less so. Even India showed little disposition to honour Gandhi's "non-violent" attitude, when faced with a threat from China. It became my own conviction and, I think, that of many others also deeply concerned, that anything like general condemnation of this or that type of weapon would lead the moralist into a morass of casuistry.

The last proposition presented for discussion in the Council's *Schema* on "The Church in the Modern World" admitted for the first time the suggestion that the Church should back up the rights of the individual conscience, as had been done, with all due safeguards, by the British Government nearly fifty years before. It was in the middle of the First World War (in 1916), and in connection with the imposition of conscription for the first time in English history, that the individual conscience received a "Magna Carta" in the admitted right of any individual to vindicate before a Tribunal a bona-fide conscientious objection. This right has survived the period between two World Wars and the whole of the Second World War. It has never been seriously attacked and never seriously abused.

The difficulty is that the countries with a historical Catholic tradition have not followed suit, either in theory or in practice. It would be unrealistic to deny that such freedom would be difficult to apply in certain cases where the principles of democracy are not accepted or even understood. Still, as it is not clear that the Christian churches could effectively do more than underwrite this individual duty of conscience, that would seem all the more reason that the Council should not be content with less.

It should be added that neither the Vatican Council nor the World Council of Churches has overlooked any of those considerations to which Mr. Berton calls attention. Thus the question which he poses about the difficulty of justifying *any* modern war, when weapons have become so devastating that both sides can be destroyed, was opened up many years ago by no less a person than Cardinal Ottaviani, now regarded as one of the *least* liberal of all the Cardinals. Yet he not only put the question but answered uncompromisingly that the outlawry of war seemed inevitable. But then, have not the United Nations, as well as groups of nations, said the same thing and even made promises in that sense?

How many of those promises have been kept? Would they have been kept any better if ecclesiastical authority – Catholic or Protestant – had intervened more decidedly? Surely it is a reasonable brake on the use of authority to respect the limits of human readiness to understand and accept its behests.

Since these questions are related to the fundamental one of the Church's relationship to the world and to the condition of man as he is (and not just as he should be), perhaps I may conclude with a few words from the declaration of his Holiness Pope Paul VI at the opening of the second session of the Vatican Council:

*May the world know that the Church looks at it with profound understanding, with a sincere admiration, sincerely disposed, not to subjugate it but to serve it, not to deprecate it but to appreciate it, not to condemn it but to sustain and save it.*

**Emil L. Fackenheim**

## 3  A JEW LOOKS AT CHRISTIANITY AND SECULARIST LIBERALISM

1  Ever since the Age of Enlightenment, Jews have had a special sense of kinship with secularist liberalism. For whereas modern Christians have often acted, and sometimes still act, as if full human rights should remain reserved for Christians, secularist liberals have consistently been in the forefront of fighters for the extension of full human rights to all men – and hence to Jews. Is it to be wondered at that even religious Jews opposed to their secularism should be drawn to their liberalism? What self-respecting modern man can accept second-class citizenship?

At the same time, even secularist-minded Jews, provided they remain Jews, find it difficult to identify themselves wholly with secularist liberalism. Throughout the ages, the choice to remain Israel has been based on a commitment to the God of Israel; and even today a Jew cannot persist in his Jewishness without hanging on to some remnants at least of his religious past. The God of Israel, however, is rejected by the secularist liberal. Moreover, He is the God shared by Jew and Christian. In the modern West, therefore, the Jew has existed and still exists between secularist liberalism and Christianity. And the conflict which has existed and still exists *between* these two ways of belief and life has contributed to a secularist-religious conflict *within* Jewish existence.

For these reasons, the Church's initiation of a dialogue with a secularist liberal is of profound concern to a Jew; and if invited to have a share in it, he does well to speak from the midst of that situation into which the history of Christian-secularist conflicts has placed him. He must try to convert the insights born of his situation into a testimony – made to both Christian and secularist liberal – to Him whom he knows as the living God.

2  The modern Church, Pierre Berton charges, stands condemned in the light of what is good in the modern world. But what is the good that he accepts and uses as overall criterion? In a Hegelian formulation, the good is what makes modern man capable of

being at home in his world; whereas pre-modern men were forced to look beyond their worlds. In the pre-modern world, the infinite value of the human person was at best the belief of a few religious groups and confined, moreover, to a passive waiting for the fulfilment of other-worldly hopes. In the modern world, it is becoming a universal rational ideal, capable of this-worldly realization. Social evils such as poverty, tyranny, the oppression of nation by nation or race by race, as well as natural evils such as starvation and want – all these might not be eliminated by modern man any more than by pre-modern man. But for modern man their elimination has become a rationally necessary ideal. He will, in fact, reduce, if not eliminate, these evils as human self-confidence combines with human social conscience to use the instruments made available by modern science. Such, in brief, is the creed of secularist liberalism.

We may as well accept from the outset the general accuracy of Pierre Berton's charge that the modern Church has sometimes opposed and at other times only belatedly supported liberal drives, and that it has rarely, if ever, spearheaded them. To quarrel with the details (and much quarrelling could be done, some in defence of the honour of Christian saints and martyrs) would only obscure a far more important question – *Why has the modern Church on the whole been lukewarm, indifferent or downright hostile to liberal drives when it might well have wholeheartedly embraced or even spearheaded them?* Or to put the same question in a still more radical and hence still more significant way: *why has the liberalism of the modern age been allowed to be shot through with a thorough-going secularist bias, when it might conceivably have been given a religious and Christian impetus?* This question is vital for the appraisal of the future of Christianity in the modern world. And it is of vital concern for the Jew as well. For it has a direct relation to the secularist-religious conflict within Jewish existence. Moreover, the secularism which has proved to be so profound a modern challenge to Christianity is no less a challenge to Judaism.

Why has modern Christianity stood over against liberalism, while Jewish existence has freely exposed itself to it, even at the price of internal conflict? For the fact of Jewish self-exposure is beyond doubt. Jews have contributed their Freuds and Einsteins far out of proportion to their numbers. They have vigorously supported liberal causes of every kind. Even when orthodox loyalty makes them hostile to one facet of the secularist-liberal creed, they are still committed to many others.

Only absurd racists would account for this Jewish behaviour in terms of some native Jewish genius for liberalism. The simple truth is that the Jew was originally made a modern liberal by his pariah status in pre-modern Christian society. If he remained a liberal when he was a pariah no more, it was because he could not forget what it was like to be a pariah, – and that there still are pariahs.

When the Jew first emerged from behind Ghetto walls the liberal ideal seemed to promise everything and threaten nothing. It threatened nothing, for all it would destroy were Ghetto walls and mediaeval oppression. It promised everything, for, to a people which had been denied liberty and equality and fraternity throughout Christendom for many centuries, the realization of these ideals was indeed bound to seem everything, or nearly everything. If, to begin with, Jews trusted the liberal promise naively it was because, thrust suddenly from mediaeval darkness into the modern world, they were dazzled by its light. Even today, however, when the darkness in the modern world has often come close to extinguishing the light, Jewish loyalty to liberal ideals remains. For the memory of past Jewish disabilities (and they are by no means all past) remains alive; and so does Jewish sympathy, strengthened by this memory, with the fate of those as yet disabled.

How, in the light of his own liberal commitments, must a Jew look on that Christian hostility and lukewarmness toward liberalism of which *The Comfortable Pew* offers such depressing evidence? If self-critical enough not to attribute Jewish liberalism to some mythical innate Jewish virtue, he will be fair enough not to attribute Christian anti-liberalism to some equally mythical Christian vice. If the one is bound up with the pre-modern experience of impotence, is not the other bound up with a pre-modern experience of power and privileged status?

The evidence, one fears, is incontrovertible. On behalf of a human equality, transcending differences not only of race, nationality, and sex but of creed as well, modern liberalism has demanded a state and society essentially secular; and Christians such as Kierkegaard have supported that demand in the name of Christianity. Yet few Christian churches have ever been quick or happy to surrender pre-modern positions close to the seats of established power, or cease to behave as though the state must somehow remain Christian, with non-Christians reduced to second-class citizenship. In the Ontario of 1965, few churches still seem much concerned with the effect on non-Christian children of Christian religious education in the public schools. And in the Canada of 1965 it still takes a fight for atheist immigrants to be granted citizenship. Indeed, such are the temptations of numbers and power that until today the Christian establishment sometimes treats even some Christians as more equal than others, and – what is more – more equal than others in the sight of God. Or so one must judge in the case of churches which are only for the rich or for whites.*

Of such behaviour Jews have frequently been the especially singled-out victims. A Jew must therefore testify that throughout the long struggle for Jewish human rights the secularist liberal has usually fought alongside the Jew, while the established Christian forces were – on the whole, but with very notable exceptions – ranged against him. No doubt much stood and still stands between the Christian as Christian and the Jew as Jew. Even so, might not Christian churches, professing as they do one Father of mankind, have matched secularist liberals (who do not profess Him) in recognizing the Jew, if as nothing else, as a full member of mankind? Yet until today even Jewish minds filled with love for the Christian faith cannot but associate two meanings with the term "Christian": commitment to a God who is Love and "Jews not wanted." Is it any wonder that modern Jews have been drawn to secularism when it alone seemed to stand for liberalism? One of the major charges a religious Jew must make against modern Christendom is that it has tempted Jews to throw in their lot with

---

*It is not overlooked, and should at this point be specifically stressed, that the synagogue too, when in the position to be tempted by numbers and power, is apt to yield to these temptations, as is illustrated by North American synagogues confined to the rich, and by the intolerance of the Jewish orthodox establishments of Great Britain and Israel of non-orthodox Jewish religious groups.

secularism, thereby turning their back on Him who is the God of both Israel and the Church.

Nor is this all. A religious Jew would be profoundly relieved had he to testify only against non-Christian forces abusing Christianity for their own purposes. (Is a "Christian" country club interested in the Christianity of its members? Or only in the exclusion of Jews from membership?) Such, however, is not the case. It is his bitter but ineluctable duty to testify against what have been official Christian teachings for many centuries, and to report clearly that even today – twenty years after Auschwitz! – few Christians have radically re-examined or turned against these teachings. The horror of Auschwitz was assuredly not a Christian but an anti-Christian responsibility. Yet would this horror have happened except for centuries of Christian teaching concerning Jewish responsibility for the crucifixion? And can one report even now that Christian self-examination has radically confronted this question with all its vast implications? Here is the view of Roy Eckhardt, a Methodist clergyman, on one such re-examination:

*In vain does one search the draft of Vatican II for even the slightest sign of Christian contrition, for even a single word of recognition that the church of Jesus Christ has been a knowing and willing participant in the centuries-long demonry of anti-semitism. If by some trick of time this schema could have been promulgated in the thirteenth century, the ideology in it would have been redeemed little. The powerful are sometimes brought to do justice to the powerless. But in the present instance, while the voices are voices which foster understanding, the hands are hands which have clasped death: the death of Christendom, the "death of God" and the death of six million Jews. How admirable of us now to exonerate the Jewish people for all their reputed transgressions! Could there be a more damning judgment upon the church of our century than this one – that not until the day after Auschwitz did Christians see fit to fabricate a correction of the record?[1]*

Nor are such criticisms of church pronouncements confined to Roman Catholicism. An Episcopalian scholar, Frederick C. Grant, assails a statement adopted by his own Protestant Episcopal House of Bishops in October 1964 (exonerating all except "some" Jews), among other reasons because, while speaking of the guilt of all men for the death of Christ, it makes no reference to any need for the church itself to repent for Christian maltreatment of Jews. "If I were a Jew," Grant writes, "I would tear up the resolution and stamp on it."[2] How many Christian theologians would even today state flatly: "A theology which consents to verbalize respecting 'Jewish responsibility for the crucifixion' – *and it does not matter which side it takes* – is not theology at all, or, if that word must be used, it is a devilish theology?" [italics ours].[3]

But to pursue that issue further would be to turn this Jewish contribution to a Christian-secularist dialogue into a contribution to a Christian-Jewish dialogue. Our main issue in this section has been Christian intolerance of the Jew, not as Jew, but as a representative of non-Christian humanity. And this section must end with a question concerning the future – a question of common Jewish-Christian concern. The present-day world is no longer white and Christian, but multi-racial and multi-religious. What will happen if secularist liberalism alone espouses clearly and without hedging the cause of man's common humanity? Unless the Church passionately embraces the liberal ideal, who will witness to this world – a world much too vast for the tiny and scattered community of Israel alone, rent as it is by its own religious-secularist conflict – who will bear witness of Him who is the living God of both Jew and Christian?

3    But what if the past Christian fear of liberal drives has been a justified fear? What if the liberal ideal threatened, not merely Christian or pseudo-Christian vested interests, but rather the very substance of the Christian faith? As science advances, must faith necessarily recede, and as modern man becomes ever more at home in this world, must God become ever more remote from it? Must a liberalism which increases human freedom in the world be a secularism which makes him self-sufficient in it – and God superfluous? We here pass beyond what has thus far separated Jews from Christians to what unites them. For the challenge posed by secularism is posed to both.

The questions we ask are not new questions. Throughout the nineteenth century secularism assumed a militant anti-religious posture, and religion, whether militant itself in the form of fundamentalism or appeasement-minded in the form of modernism, was on the defensive. Far from being new, our questions may well seem by now wholly outmoded. For in twentieth-century North America, militancy and warfare have given way to mutual tolerance and dialogue. Yet in a true dialogue one must closely inspect what is offered by the partner. And to judge by what *The Comfortable Pew* offers to Christianity, the old warfare may well be preferable to the new tolerance.

Can a Christian believer accept Berton's "reverent agnosticism"? What would he then have that non-believers lack? Surely there is no Christian monopoly on the belief that "truth is better than a lie, honesty better than a deceit, love and mercy better than hate and mistrust." True, non-Christians would not accept these "general principles" on the authority of the "founder" of Christianity. But this, far from making the Christian superior to the secularist liberal, might actually make him inferior. For the secularist liberal might claim, as Kant long ago did, that he can dispense with all external authorities, because the general principles of morality dwell in his heart. Clearly, a "reverent agnosticism" prepared to say to *all* questions "because of the limitations of my mind and the nature of the subject, I cannot know the final answer" is poles apart from a faith which moves mountains. And this alone would surely be enough to make Berton's peace-offer religiously unacceptable.

Matters are made worse because Berton himself does not, after all, leave *all* questions open. The questions not open are those to which secularist liberalism has the answer. And the final upshot is that Berton's "new-look-Christianity" would reduce itself to a willing tool in the pursuit of the goals of secularist liberalism. But can there be peace at such a price? Can any Christian reduce his faith to a mere cure for human weakness, and his God to a mere instrument of human purposes however worth while?

Is this the best shape in which Christianity can emerge from radical self-exposure to the modern world? Rather than accept the word of a secularist, one must surely first look at actual Christian self-exposures. And one must state bluntly that *The Comfortable Pew* has not looked closely, thereby giving a scandalously one-sided picture of Christian realities. The book dwells rightly on the conservatism of Christian establishments. It says little of way-out

Christian radicals, anti-Nazi Christian resistance fighters, or the critical thought which has existed in the Church for well over a century. To charge that such stirrings have had much too limited an effect on established Christian institutions or the general Christian consciousness would have been one thing. Virtually to ignore them is quite another.

It must be admitted that most nineteenth-century Christian self-exposures to liberal and critical ideas were half-hearted, apologetic, and lacking in complete integrity; and for this reason alone, perhaps, foredoomed to ineffectiveness. Thus while nineteenth-century fundamentalists would attack the theory of evolution, their modernist contemporaries would accept it – and promptly find a religious meaning in it! Or (to give another example) Protestant biblical scholars would subject the Old Testament to a purportedly objective criticism, yet make its inferiority to the New Testament a foregone conclusion – a practice deserving the remark that "the higher criticism is the higher anti-semitism."

But present-day self-exposure to the challenge of liberalism and criticism in significant quarters of the Church cannot be said to suffer from such shortcomings. Here "demythologizing" is the word of the hour, and it is apparently carried on without set limits. Secular man with his concerns is the man of the hour; it is by his standards that Christian faith is to measure its relevance. And among the theological heroes are Marx and Nietzsche. Nor are these stirrings only theoretical or academic; witness the sit-ins in Mississippi and Alabama, and the sales of *Honest to God* or, for that matter, of *The Comfortable Pew*. Never in history has Christian self-exposure to the secular world and all its works been so radical, honest, and fearless of consequence.

Indeed, if self-exposure to the modern world were all that mattered, one would have to be wholly satisfied with the quality if not the quantity of these stirrings. But if the *Christian* quality of this self-exposure matters as well, one must have a sense of uneasiness. This Christian self-exposure is much needed and much delayed, hence impatient and turbulent. Could it be that it does not always know what it is doing? Is there no danger that the present "religionless Christians" will reject, along with the pseudo-gods whom Marx and Nietzsche destroyed, the true God whom these heroes of theirs defied? Demythologizing is a necessity, and a God "up there" is an outdated metaphor. But may a Christian say the same of a God "out there" – pictured spatially outside man because other-than-human?* It is more than four decades since Karl Barth and Martin Buber first pointed out the vast difference between a radically open Christian or Jewish encounter with the world, and surrender to the world, a surrender made wholesale because presupposing the world's standards. One sometimes feels today that their lesson must be stated and thought through all over again.

Coming from a Jew, this warning may seem to have a strange source. To the Christian it must often seem that Jewish interest in Christianity is confined to the growth of liberal attitudes in it; and that if these attitudes foster a secularism that undermines the Christian faith Jews are not much worried. Yet, we have advisedly said earlier that Jews have existed between secularist liberalism and Christianity since the rise of the modern age; and we must now add that events in this century have done much to produce conscious Jewish awareness of this condition.

Religious Jews, at any rate, might have felt some uneasiness with secularist liberalism in the very period, immediately following the French revolution, which was instrumental in proclaiming their emancipation. The revolution, in a famous phrase, would "grant to the Jew as man everything, and to the Jew as Jew nothing." But who was here doing the granting and denying? Sovereign man. And what sacrifice did he demand of the Jew? Part of what had been his relation to God. For two good reasons, however, little uneasiness was felt at the time. First, man, though sovereign, was not absolute sovereign; the domain of private conscience remained untouched, and the Jew, bidden to become a man abroad, was permitted to remain a Jew at home. Secondly, the man who was sovereign was Universal Man – the core of the secularist liberal creed even today; and who could not give some considerable loyalty to Universal Man?†

---

*Cf. John A. T. Robinson, *Honest to God*, SCM Press 1963, chapters 2 and 3. Our few remarks are of course no adequate response to Bishop Robinson's earnest and thoughtful book.

†Enlightenment ideas still have a strong and beneficial hold on the Anglo-Saxon mind. Thus the doctrine that all men are created equal is of the

But there soon began in continental Europe two ominous and interrelated developments. Universal Man became a particular man – the man of modern nationalism. And this man had religious, or rather pseudo-religious, pretensions. His voice (especially, but not exclusively, in Germany) became ever more strident, and the realm reserved for private conscience ever more precarious. In the end, Nazism made the national state total, destroyed the realm of private conscience, demanded absolute conformity, and murdered Jews.

Such has been the contemporary Jew's experience with a secularism become deified, all-encompassing, demonic and mad. A Jew can hardly bear to transform this experience into testimony. For it is a tragedy unequalled in all of Israel's tear-stained history; and, having been singled out as no other group of men, he must fear that few non-Jews will understand his testimony. Yet out of the midst of tragedy, must he not warn today's Christian against surrender, however well-intentioned, to *any* secularism, however far removed from Nazism? Would not such Christian surrender be an invitation to secularism to appropriate the vacated religious sphere, thus becoming what Jews and Christians have always known as idolatry?

It would of course be absurd to hold all secularism responsible for Nazi madness – as absurd as to try to inspire a "return to religion" by issuing dire warnings of the danger of its recurrence. Secularist liberals are foes of Nazism. And Nazi "paganism" is not cause for Christian self-congratulation but much rather for such agonised self-appraisals as *The Deputy*.

---

very life-blood of the United States, and the doctrine of the separation of State and Church is a virtual reality even where it is not, as in the United States, a formal constitutional principle. Christians sometimes assail this latter doctrine, as a product of secularism. The contrast with the example of Germany might make them wonder whether, protect as it does *both* Church and State from mutual intrusion, it is not much rather the product of a sensitive religious conscience. They might also wonder whether, rather than look for opportunities of invasion of the State by the Church, they would not be better employed to safeguard the Church against intrusion from the State, an end best, if in the end not solely, accomplished by a sensitive religious conscience. But that such conscience must find expression in secular action is the main burden of this article.

Even so, the Nazi experience (and not it alone) forces Jewish and Christian believers to raise one fundamental question. The world which demands their involvement is complex. Only rarely, as with racial justice, is the stand required straightforward. On most issues they cannot easily be sure of what is morally required, or protect themselves against giving unwitting support to all sorts of dubious forces. One special question above all must be asked: *What is the firm ground of faith on which they may stand as they try to meet the demands of the world?* What may they *bring to* the world, lest self-exposure end up with total surrender?

There is no easy answer. Still, Christian behaviour under the Nazi trial furnishes one invaluable lesson. Throughout the nineteenth century, modernist Christian thought had been in search of easy adjustments. What if criticism did reduce the word of God to that of man! Was not the human word the product of creative culture, hence itself divine? Thus a process of Christian surrender began, the more thorough when the deified human word was national or fascist. Much German Protestantism had been "German-Christian" long before the advent of Nazism. And when the word of Hitler became the word of God it offered little or no resistance.

Contrast Hitler's German-Christian church with the German Confessional church. Its subsequent leaders – notably Karl Barth – had been forced to question modernist compromises during the first war, when clergymen of every warring nation had claimed the Christian God on behalf of their national causes. This was worship, not of a God immanent in culture, but of a deified culture against God. And it demanded – after demythologizing had done all its necessary work – the reaffirmation of the *distinction* between the word of God and the word of man. It demanded that man, rather than idolize his human concerns, stand before Him who is the Judge of states and cultures – and of churches and liberal ideals. When the Nazi trial occurred, it found few Christians prepared. But the few prepared were prepared well. They were not tempted to deify the voice of either their nation or its leader. Indeed, they knew that, precisely because the voice of this leader made claims to divinity, it was the voice of the Antichrist.

Such has been the ground on which some contemporary Christians have stood, in the very midst of a multitude eager to mount swastikas on the spires of Christian churches. But is the ground a firm ground? Can the modern believer – Jew or Christian – *bring* the word of God *to* the modern world, even as he exposes himself to it freely and without reservation?

4    Here it is at long last time to bear direct witness to Him who has been the God of Israel for more than three millennia, and the God of the Christian church since its inception. *He is the One who is infinite, yet relates Himself to finite man; who in His power does not need man, yet in His love chooses to need him; who in His self-sufficiency does not require the world yet wishes to require it – and bids man do His will in it.*

Such a God does not require demythologizing. He already *is* demythologized, and has been so ever since He first revealed Himself in an infinity destructive of all finite idols. (Only the images man forms of Him require demythologizing, but even these are already *recognized* as being mere images.) Nor does a man whom such a God has singled out have to be turned to the world; he already *is* turned to the world, by a God who bids him work in it. Such a man, moreover, does not need to learn of human freedom; he is already given such knowledge by an infinite God who has accepted him in his finite humanity and made man ruler over the earth. Nor, finally, must such a man still rise above a parochialism which would accept the humanity of one group of men but deny that of others. He is already raised above it, by a God who reveals Himself as the God of all men, even as He is present to one group of men.

Such, in brief, is the testimony. And it must be made first to the secularist liberal, so as to embrace his liberalism and repudiate his secularism. The infinite value of the human person, always part of both Jewish and Christian faith, must now by faith be accepted as a rational ideal, if by "rational" and "ideal" is meant a goal demanding secular realization – by and on behalf of all men. And in accepting this demand, modern Jew and Christian must descend into this secular world, from what has often been, and sometimes still is, a remote Heaven. Yet in this very descent they must refuse to grant that God is absent from this world, or that, reduced to a finite presence in a finite world, He is Himself finite.

In this refusal, they must confront the secularist liberal with a direct challenge. Like Jew and Christian, he would assert the infinite value of the human person. But how can finite man possess such a value when he is cut off from the infinite God? And how can the secularist liberal defend it against anti-liberal secularists who threaten it? On one side secularism would reduce all human value to mere finiteness, thus making all human persons mere means to supposedly higher ends. And on another it would raise to pseudo-infinity some finite values – true values such as talent or acomplishment or false values such as colour of skin – thus making some men the slaves of others. Can the secularist liberal resist such anti-liberal, secularist pressures? And if he can and does, could it be because of a genuine, albeit hidden, commitment to Him who is God of Israel and the Church? Might it conceivably be the case that, if the modern secularist liberal ever did become a secularist, it was in the end only because of the inveterate anti-liberalism of the established religious forces?

At this point, what may begin as a Jewish or Christian testimony against the secularist liberal must inexorably turn into, and culminate in, Jewish and Christian self-criticism. How could either believer ever have been indifferent, lukewarm, or hostile to the liberal ideal – and this in the name of their faith! – when that ideal is the most authentic modern secular expression of their faith? How could they ever have feared the free scientific exploration of the world when, long freed of idolatrous worship of the world, they should have been the freest of all scientific explorers? Why afraid of technology, when they were the first to believe that the earth is handed over to human rule? Above all else, how could any Jew or Christian who ever believed in one Father of all men have failed to rally to the modern struggle on behalf of man's common humanity, or have sabotaged secularists who led this struggle?

The answer to all these questions is surely not faith, but lack of faith; not confidence in a God present in the modern, no less than in the pre-modern, world, but rather the fear that this God, present no longer, must become in the modern world a pious but lifeless memory. Mixed with the fear of His absence, is there a fear of His presence? The fear that God might be present to judge Church and Synagogue in their unrepentant failure to be open to both Word and world – open to the word which is "like a fire . . . a hammer that breaketh the rock in pieces" (Jer. 23:29), open to the world into which they are commissioned to "bring good tidings to the poor . . . to bind up the brokenhearted, to proclaim liberty to the captives and the opening of the prisons to them that are bound"? (Isa. 61:1, quoted Luke 4:18-19.) One cannot doubt that this unbelief and fear is a cause – if not *the* cause – of the tragic modern split between those who espouse the cause of men but reject the God who first espoused it, and those who, seeking to espouse God's cause, are in flight from the modern world and thus from real men.

Is the hour too late for the healing of this split? Not if the ancient promise is true, the promise which was given through the mouth of Joshua: "Have not I commanded thee? Be strong and of a good courage; be not afraid, neither be thou dismayed; for the Lord thy God is with thee whithersoever thou goest." (Josh. 1:9.)

# FIVE

# THE UNCOMFORTABLE FEW

THE UNCOMFORTABLE FEW: A PROPHECY

*by Lotte and Werner Pelz*

*Werner Pelz was born and educated in Berlin and Lotte Pelz in Vienna. She is a teacher, and he has been the Vicar of an Anglican Church in Bolton, England. Both of them contribute frequently to such magazines as* The Guardian, the Church Times, The Listener *and* Theology. *Their best-known book is* God is No More, *a prophetic attack on religion in the light of the Biblical vision of God and man.*

## Lotte & Werner Pelz

# THE UNCOMFORTABLE FEW:
# A PROPHECY

We who are also trying to find the "something" of great price that so many – believers and unbelievers alike – still, surprisingly, expect to find hidden somewhere behind or beyond religion, cannot help agreeing with almost every one of the accusations Pierre Berton hurls at the ecclesiastical set-up. There is, however, a quaint, old-world look about the arguments of one so eager to drag the church from the bronze into the aluminum-plastic age, to make it play its cymbals, lutes, and harps before microphones, T.V. cameras and newspaper editors. Surely his objections have been stated 50, 100, even 200 years ago and have not substantially increased in depth and acumen since the days of Voltaire. One is a little disappointed in Mr. Berton for having missed an opportunity, for having apparently forgotten – like many other objectors and defenders – to re-read Nietzsche, Marx, Jeremiah, Isaiah, and that much misunderstood Man of Nazareth who, during the last 2500 years, have attacked religion on a much profounder level. Perhaps one should not blame Mr. Berton, but the Christians who have forced this superficiality of attack on their attackers.

Since the Enlightenment, Christians have usually taken one of two ways. On the one hand they have built barricades, shaken the fist under the nose of whatever the spirit of the age might have been, insisted that the Church or the Bible or Luther or Calvin or Wesley were right, and all the worse for the world if it did not acknowledge it. Or, on the other hand, they have tried to become sweetly reasonable, attempted to identify Christianity with everything good and kind and humane – and, since Kierkegaard, also with everything serious and ultimate and "real" – to disencumber themselves of the heavy particularity of a heritage that had lost its sex-appeal; to turn the tables on all respectable unbelievers – insinuating that, knowing or unknowing, they were already "one of us." These two ways continually diverge and converge, often in the same personality, and this criss-crossing of not always clearly distinguished tendencies – now to preserve, defend, make sure, be certain; now to move with the times, keep in touch, demythologize – creates a tense and yet listless atmosphere of bewilderment, awkwardness and futility. It leads to the disconcerting wavering between a half-hearted fanaticism and a self-conscious broad-mindedness. It lures the academic into endless exploration of artificial ambiguities, which prevent him from noticing that he has avoided the fundamentally much more ambiguous position into which all those are thrown who have been bitten by the bug that bit the prophets and poets of the Old and New Testaments.

The Jewish prophetic tradition begins, Homer-like, with the early, epic compilers of the Pentateuch and runs in a straight if broken line up to the Joshua whom the Greeks called Jesus.*

Before we can hope to make sense of it, we have to purge our mind of any tendency to identify its Yahweh (Jehovah) with what we have got into the habit of calling "God." We meet this Yahweh making a man by blowing his very own aspiration, spirit, breath into a lump of mud. He surrounds his creature with solicitude and

---

*May we stress from the outset that we are consciously concentrating on the "prophetic" tradition. It will be objected that Old and New Testament also enshrine what may be called loosely a "priestly" tradition which – it is usually implied – balances the prophetic excesses of enthusiasm. We cannot deny this fact, nor that the final shape of the Bible and the fact that it has come to be accepted as the "Holy Bible" is a "priestly" work. We do, however, insist that already in the biblical documents the reader is asked to make a choice. Throughout the Old Testament the cleavage can still be felt, in spite of hundreds of years of harmonizing priestly editing. (Compare the figure of Moses with that of Aaron, Deuteronomy with Leviticus, Isaiah 40:55 with Ezra and Nehemiah; see also Amos 7:10-17; Isaiah 1:12-17; Jeremiah 7; the book of Jonah.) But while the Old Testament may leave us in some doubt, the New does not. The final confrontation of priest and prophet – not perhaps historically correct, but parabolically pointed – reveals the necessity of choice: Caiphas or Jesus, the wisdom of the world, of the statesman, the responsible religious leader or the quixotic wisdom that claims to have overcome the world and uses the world merely as the yet-to-be-formed.

In the following we are not going to make any distinction between legendary and historical material. We do not claim to know where the one ends and the other begins, not even in connection with the prophet of Nazareth. But we do believe that the Bible as a whole wants to be treated as legend, as parable; that it rather indiscriminately uses any kind of material in order to convey a concern, a most peculiar view.

then throws him – and her – out of his garden for infringing an arbitrary rule. He floods the world and afterwards "repents." He chooses the Jews – a preference Christians have never been able to make their own – and rejects the Egyptians. He chooses, only to be doubly exacting with the chosen. This Yahweh – as Job knew – is responsible for the poverty of the righteous, the riches of the wicked, the perversity of rulers, for cancer and earthquake, for pain and death, as well as for the crocodile and the idyllic hippopotamus, the horse and the mountain goat, and for the general state of things as they are, giving some people every reason for bitter complaint and some, the "sons of God," the desire to shout for joy. Finally, Yahweh becomes identified with the elusive King-Father-Master figure of the parables of Jesus.

Yahweh is a restlessly ambiguous figure or anti-figure. He is as mysterious and slippery, as comfortable and callous, as generous and demanding as life itself. It is the surprising accomplishment of the prophets – achieved with such lightness of touch that we have hardly yet recognized it as an achievement – to have twisted the very arbitrariness of life into the likeness of man's aspiration.

Yahweh is also the dream life engenders, the intense wish-dream that *will* impose itself on reality, *will* importune the future until it yield what the past seems to have promised. The whole Old Testament hangs between Paradise, always remembered as lost, and the Promised Land, the promising future, ever receding yet always teasing us with the possibility of fulfillment, of making true what we had hoped for once and had betrayed when we decided to become "realistic." The Old Testament insinuates into our distracted hearts the sense that nostalgia and longing are more "real" than anything we do not long for – however "real" it may be. If there is anything that distinguishes man from beast, it is our power to dream and our obstinate endeavours to translate the dream into something tangible. In this effort we never altogether succeed, we never altogether fail. But *while* we are engaged in it, we realize that the wish-dream is the maker of the man, the creator of the human world.

Dream is movement, restlessly playing round everything that merely is: like the sculptor's fingers round the stone to be shaped; like the lover's hand over the body of the beloved, always discovering everything anew; like the poet's fancy over everything he has experienced, the inventor's thought round an insoluble problem, the gardener's hoe restlessly keeping the jungle at bay. Everything that is or has already been accomplished, is merely a starting point, is dust for the making of bricks, for the building of new castles in Spain; it is the opportunity for inspiration. The followers of Yahweh are those who find dreams more convincing than what the compact majority has been taught to understand as reality. The followers of Yahweh are those who are capable of leaving everything that is solid, secure, and measurable to go wholeheartedly after what they cannot help loving better than security and solidity.

Think of Abraham, the old man, who turns from all he knows and has, towards the promise of what he knows and has not yet; of Jacob who plots and plans and cheats for the sake of the immaterial "something" which alone makes things significant – like the beauty of a girl's face. Think of Moses who infected a whole people with his dream; of Amos who faced the economic and social realities of his day with his breathtaking utopian vision, convinced that the vision was real and reality a dream soon to be scattered. Jeremiah thought that the city whose dream had been ossified into temple worship had already condemned itself to death; but he also believed that the power of a new vision could rebuild what all realistic efforts could not save from oblivion. In Deutero-Isaiah the dream bulges into the proportions of the universe itself, at the very moment when "reality" seems to have proved conclusively that all realistic expectations are vanity of vanities. But the prophets also knew that Yahweh is known only *in* the dreaming, in the unremitting endeavour to let the vision transfigure the mud of our conditioning, to wrest a "blessing" from the very inevitability of the inevitable. The moment I want to investigate the reality, the existence of Yahweh, he has already withdrawn like a dream on waking.

Yahweh is experienced as the maker, enthuser, seducer of the "single-one": he does not create mankind but *a* man, *a* woman. He carries one man and his family through the universal flood. Out of the confusion of imperial ambitions, he calls one old man, simply to live his life to the full, to start it again when it seems almost over, to live as if there were only life. Yahweh is the inspiration, the accomplice of the man who realizes he cannot get what he really desires by "honest" means.* I experience what the prophets called Yahweh, when I am torn out of my anonymity by the intensity of my vision, when I am made separate and single-minded by that vision.

Yet he who is singled out by the prophetic spirit – to be artist, reformer, lover, explorer – is singled out for the sake of the others. He is to be an aspiration and inspiration, a blessing and a parable, to anyone among the many who has ears to hear and who, touched by his example, wants to become a "single-one" in turn. All the families of the earth were to be blessed in Abraham. Through him every man is reminded of the possibility of living his own single life to the full, even when it seems too late. Joseph, always attentive to the mysterious message of the dream, is made very rich in order to make many rich. Moses is inspired by an enthusiasm strong enough to inspire a whole people, to make of the many – the much-too-many, the slaves, the mere perpetuators of "things-as-they-are" – a community of single-minded ones: "I wish all Yahweh's People were prophets." In Moses the tension and ambiguity of being inspired by Yahweh becomes very clear: he has seen; the vision has overwhelmed him. He says: "Yahweh, you have deceived me, and I was deceived; you are stronger than I. Now I want everyone to see, everyone to be responsive." But everyone cannot see, until he has ceased being "everyone" and has become an Abraham, Jacob, Moses, a single-one, very distinct from everyone. All Moses could do was to lure "everyone" into the wilderness, where everyone perished, except Joshua and Caleb, two single-ones. Was his vision true? And if it was, was it not terrible? Is he not terrifying, this Yahweh who is what he is, has mercy on whom he will have mercy? Yet the figure of Moses became the prophetic parable par excellence. Amos, Micah, Isaiah, Jeremiah, Ezekiel, reflect his archetypal experience: called and sent, chosen and commissioned, inspired to inspire, they call everyman into the intensity of their dream. They speak to everyman, knowing that everyman will hear and not understand, see

---

*cf. the parable of the Unjust Steward, the Treasure in the Field. Also the Prodigal Son who does not go home because he is sorry, but because he is hungry; yet will not say that but; "Father, I have sinned . . ." for he knows it will make a better impression.

and not comprehend, will become more and more obstinate in his realism. Yet they cannot help speaking and acting in the hope that among everyman there may be the one who, inspired in turn, will himself become the new prophet, the remnant.

The prophetic spirit makes a man absolutely responsible. It persuades him that he can prevail against overwhelming odds, as long as he continues to believe precisely this against all possible doubt, continues to hope against the most real and reasonable despair.

Joshua or Jesus of Nazareth is the last of this long succession of visionaries. He cannot be isolated, cannot be understood apart from them. He is the heir of this unique tradition of quixotic utopianism, of a quietly arrogant aristocracy of the spirit, of absurd hopefulness and expectancy, of intense commitment to the "not-yet," the ever-moving, invisible, the yet-to-be-incarnated, Yahweh Who is what He is and will be. In Jesus the various strands of Yahweh-apprehension – of which we have unravelled a few – have become woven into a pattern.

The Yahweh that lurks behind his parables is at least as elusive and arbitrary as the inspirer of Moses, the deceiver of Jeremiah, the tormentor of Job. Here he scatters wholesale and regardless; there he spring-cleans the whole house to retrieve a lost dollar. Now he falls round the neck of a returning scoundrel, now he chases a faithful, if timid, servant into the outer darkness which will obviously prove too much for him. He goes after one sheep and lets multitudes go to the devil. He rejects the righteous, accepts sinners, lets the sun rise over both. He praises the cheat for his cleverness and turns his wrath on the respectable people who have more responsible things to do than go to a party. He forgives the man who owes him more than one thinks a man can ever owe, and bangs the door shut on some thoughtless girls for being five minutes late. He takes from those that have not, and gives to those that have. He looks after each sparrow, numbers each hair, but will not save the single one, the son, who has taken upon himself the whole precariousness of being a single one and being single-minded.*

---

*From here we can see once again, that the biblical vision cannot be summed up as "moral religion" or "religion of love." Yahweh is jealous,

As Yahweh had called Abraham, Moses, and the prophets out of the cosiness of the city, out of the glorious achievement of the kingdom, out of the security of anonymity; so Jesus calls his followers out of business and family – into the bird-free existence of what he called a "kingdom," sponging on others who stuck it out; he calls them out of the temple and the synagogue, out of the political cross-currents of his age, and makes them responsible for a never-to-be-accomplished, always-to-be-attempted "kingdom." His "Lord," "Father," "God" is again the ever-moving who turns all achievement to dust and makes much out of almost nothing, out of the one, the grain of mustard seed. And if you have of faith, i.e., of Yahweh-passion, Yahweh-inspiration, as little as a grain of mustard seed, you can say to this mountain . . .

In his temptation parable – the most ambiguous summing up of his most ambiguous intentions – Jesus insinuates that he has opted for the dream against mere reality. He refuses to bribe, to coerce, to prove anything, i.e., to use economic, technical, political, or metaphysical means or arguments in order to persuade, to be "realistic" or objective. He does not want men to be dependent on him, to be obeyed or revered. He proffers no security, no certainty, no sign. He seems to have desired only one thing: to become the incarnation of his vision, the expression of his dream; to be re-membered as one who made of his life, even his death, a legend, a parable that would encourage others to believe that they too could remain faithful to their vision against the overwhelming

---

often vindictive, always biased. When therefore a prophet like Hosea or Deutero-Isaiah or, later on, the writer of I John say or imply that "God is love," they do not point to an "ultimate reality," certainly not to something fairly obvious. They are engaged in the typical Jewish prophetic activity of twisting the inevitable's tail, of affirming an absurd "in spite of." They also reveal their own adventurousness of spirit by accepting the very openness and insecurity of "what will be" as the invitation, the opportunity, to trust and risk and to create – and, sometimes, even to love. For they knew that love, to be genuine and spontaneous, has to be the overflow of an altogether more fundamental response to life. It has first of all to be a love of life itself. Neither can Jesus' teaching be condensed into the word love – which word has been made to cover a multitude of intellectual sins ever since the Church found itself on the defensive. No, it may be altogether more moral, more loving, more democratic *not* to be a Christian.

pressure of politics, society, religion, and the general fatefulness of things – including death. In all this He insists quite simply that a man will find what he really longs for, in following what seems promising to him and not in hanging on – no matter for what good reasons – to whatever he has already found uninspiring. (Yes, the prophetic message is at heart so simple and awful and tautologous. We all understand it. We all think it is true. We all are afraid it is not. We all know that we cannot know for sure until it is too late.)

Joshua acknowledges the prophetic spirit as man's most promising inspiration. He calls this elusive, wilful, evasive, and implacable spirit "Father, Abba," because it makes a man as responsible for the world as an heir is for his father's estate. "Be *you* therefore perfect – merciful – even as your Father in heaven is perfect – merciful."

More even than the prophets of the Old Testament, Jesus is responsible. *They* still said: "Thus says Yahweh." *He* says: "I say to you." He takes upon himself the prerogatives of Yahweh. He forgives, heals, restores, transfigures the law. He takes it upon Himself when and how to die. The Gospel of John is an incisive elaboration of Jesus' self-estimate, or rather of His estimate of the significance of the self, the "I." And Jesus' uniqueness subsists in having insisted on the uniqueness of every man who has the courage to say: "I am I. I am responsible." His inspiration comes to life in me when I have the temerity to say: "Before Abraham was, I am. I am the good shepherd, the door, the bread, the wine, the light – for if I am not, *nobody* is; if I am not, I am nothing. I and my vision are one. He who has seen me has seen what I have seen. I have overcome what overcomes everybody."

Jesus especially impressed on his first disciples that they would do greater things even than he. (This thought rather than any artificial humility, could be the measure of our failure.)

Jesus calls the few for the sake of the many, me for the sake of all. He does it in the clear knowledge that there will always be only the few who can hear *and* understand. It may even be good that it is so, for if the salt fills the whole plate . . . if there is only light . . . Jesus set out to encourage those few who get excited about the "impossible possibilities" of the beast-angel man and are ready to shoulder their responsibility for the reshaping of "reality" into a similitude of their dream. He makes himself – and me by implication – responsible beyond death – "heaven and earth will pass away; my words will not pass away" – and so intensifies my desire to make of my life – if must be, even my death – a legend, a parable that will always speak.

When I have been bitten by the prophetic bug, I cannot help confirming in what I say, think, and do that I too have been moved by what had once moved the quixotic Jewish visionaries. I naturally want to say: Those men have enlarged my mind, have given to my awareness of the world a new dimension of wonder, to my awareness of myself a new intensity and hopefulness. They have done for me what Beatrice did for Dante, Marx for Lenin, what a particularly pretty pearl had once done for a particularly foolish merchant.

Then I, too, want to prophesy. I want to impress everyone with the universality and urgency of my hope and longing and nostalgia. And at the same time I shall know that I can never know whether I am right to trouble others, whether I am not a deceiver as well as deceived. I shall want to change what is and shall know that even should I succeed, it will have to be changed again. I shall, like the artist, want everyman to see what I have seen. I shall want no man to see *as* I see, to see eye to eye with me. I shall expect any man, at any moment, to become a prophet to me, to inspire and deceive me.

This is the ambiguity of the Yahweh-inspired life. There will, most likely, never be more than the uncomfortable few who want to live it, who want to leave behind the comfortable dreamlessness of religious, social, political, or anti-religious institutions or isms; who will embark on the high endeavour of making all the world acknowledge their Dulcinea as a most beautiful lady; who know that only in trying to express fully their most peculiar and particular self, can they hope to become a parable, a legend of universal significance. But these few will continue to wait and work for the day – the day of Yahweh – when each man will reach the stature of his desire.

# SIX

# HOW TO LIVE IN THE SECULAR CITY: TWO VIEWS

I

AN OPEN LETTER TO THE CHURCH
*by Arnold Edinborough*

2

AN INTERVIEW WITH HARVEY COX

*Arnold Edinborough is editor of* Saturday Night, *Canada's leading monthly journal. He is a prolific lecturer, a lively critic of contemporary life, a prominent Anglican layman and a columnist in* The Canadian Churchman.

*Harvey G. Cox, a professor at the Harvard Divinity School, is the author of* The Secular City, *a stimulating book which may well be one of the most important theological works of our time. What follows here is an excerpt from an interview with Jack Rutherford of the* CBC. *The full interview was broadcast on the* CBC *radio program* Christian Frontiers, *in October, 1965, and portions of it are contained in one of the* CBC *contributions to the internation television series* Intertel. *This is a program about the Christian church's dialogue with the world which is being broadcast in many countries during 1966.*

# 1 AN OPEN LETTER TO THE CHURCH

It is a sad but undeniable fact that the Church no longer communicates with the modern world. If it did the world would be much more aware of what the Church is and what it does, and much less impressed by such books as *The Comfortable Pew*. But it is not just the outside world with which the Church has lost touch. It seems to me as an insider that it has lost contact with many of its own people as well.

How does the Church talk to its faithful?

On any Sunday morning in suburban Canada an Anglican Church will be full of young parents and young children. They want to be there; they are looking for something from the Church, and the children are there at the adults' service so that they can, in the words of one clergyman I know, learn a sense of reverence and become aware of the beauty of the liturgy.

Remember that these people watch four or five hours of television a day; they read one or maybe two newspapers a day; they are enmeshed in the most complex web of advertising messages man has ever devised – messages deliberately compounded of elements which by research have proved their capacity to persuade or shock.

To this group, the minister moves forward and says: "Dearly beloved brethren, the Scripture moveth us in sundry places to acknowledge and confess our manifold sins and wickedness." Could anything be more inept? Could any form of words communicate less?

I know that the liturgy is a noble work of man and God. I know that there are great, rolling, sonorous phrases which lap us all in a warm sense of well-being and emotional uplift. I admit that I can never say, "We do not presume to come to this Thy table, O merciful Lord, trusting in our own righteousness . . ." without feeling profoundly moved. But I, most of the clergy, and a very small percentage of the laity have had special instruction and training in Elizabethan English. But how an insurance executive or a plumber or an advertising salesman can be expected to get anything out of it, I fail to see.

It may be argued, of course, that there is a supra-communication going on here which is too deep for words, and that long familiarity with the liturgy induces a proper other-worldly, non-literal attitude and reverence towards God in His house. Even if one admits that – which I do not – then why does the Church stick to this same sixteenth century phraseology on the occasions when it is supposed to be communicating at the literal level? Why, for example, in a prayer-book revised in 1959, are clergy instructed to read twice a year without fail an exhortation about Holy Communion which begins: "Dearly Beloved in the Lord, ye that mind to come to the Holy Communion in the Body and Blood of our Saviour Christ must consider how St. Paul exhorteth all persons diligently to try and examine themselves," etc.

Well, I can hear people saying, "What do we do – throw out the whole liturgy? Write it all in modern English like the new English Bible?", to which I answer, "Why not?" This is what the Roman Catholic Church has done. They have, in one magnificent gesture, delivered their people from the incantatory music of Latin to the blunt personal reminder in English of what being a Christian means. And if we don't want to do that, if we insist on retaining those glorious rolling periods of Elizabethan English, we must be prepared at least to teach people how to appreciate their meaning and magic power. This must, in fact, become an immediate concern.

That the laity feels strongly about the need for a recasting of both the form and manner of our weekly worship, was shown strongly at the Canadian Church's General Synod of September, 1965. In the course of three days, laymen moved or seconded motions which called for "the preparation of a version of the present Book of Common Prayer in contemporary English"; urged "diocesan bishops to permit various exploratory liturgical uses in their dioceses"; got approval for a new hymn-book which will include, among other things, some attempt to use the vocabulary and the art forms of the twentieth century. All these motions were passed unanimously, and a message from the House of Bishops which declined to "authorize" the New English Bible for reading in church was rejected by the Lower House.

I hope that these changes in liturgy, hymnary, and scripture can be made soon, because if church people hear in contemporary language what it is they have been praying for and assenting to for years, this could quicken their faith into something worth communicating to people outside the Church.

But what about the outsiders? Will they be persuaded that Christianity is worth a second look (or even a first one)? Can we convince them that the love of God and the service of Christ are not just in-group activities but ones which have a direct bearing on their daily lives and on their deepest concerns?

We shall not reach them just by talking, however many bright parsons we put on radio hot-lines, however many religious talks or services are carried on television. We have to do it by example. To live one's faith is ultimately the only argument for it. And this means not only the practice of the law of love in the most important of our relationships with other persons, but a whole host of difficult lesser acts of honesty and justice in the most casual or distant or impersonal of relationships as well – in refusing unethical business involvements, for example; in challenging the spread of malicious gossip; in driving one's car in a charitable way, in making honest income tax returns to the welfare state (itself largely the creation of the Western Christian conscience).

It means that when I hear people are living in slums and that these slums have been created by ruthless land speculators, I – not somebody else – must help the people and eradicate the evil. I – not somebody else – am required to appear before City Council to argue on their behalf; I – not somebody else – am required to urge my alderman to appoint relocation officers and to review the zoning and housing by-laws.

If I do it in my parish, others will follow. If the parish does it, other parishes will follow. When a group of parishes concentrate on a particular area, the city takes note. When one city takes note, others take note.*

---

*Lest this all seem very abstract and only an indication of what might happen, let me say that though the "I" in this case is not I, yet the parish is my parish of St. Simon-the-Apostle, Toronto. And now five parishes of three different denominations are not only working to relieve the present suffering, but a joint committee is working closely with City Hall politicians and officials to see that the creation of such a slum cannot happen again.

If I can see what is happening on my own doorstep, and my personal responsibility for it, I shall be led to see what is happening beyond it. If I protest the idiotic laws about birth control in Canada, for example, I shall be moved to recognize the need for birth control information in Africa and India – and to see my share of the responsibility for the burden of poverty and suffering that exists there.

In Canada, we are sitting on top of the biggest pile of natural resources in the world: food, power, water, metals, and minerals. As Christians we say that they are gifts from God and that they must be shared. Yet we hoard them while people are starving to death in India. We subsidize farmers in Canada so that they can store their grain while people are growing up deformed in Africa through vitamin deficiency. We convert butter to butter oil because it is easier to keep that way though we have thirty million pounds in storage now. And still the pitiful appeals for help come – through the Primate's World Relief Fund, the Save the Children Fund, the Oxford Committee for Famine Relief.

In the face of the world's inequalities we must see that Christianity in our century means a complete reassessment of the second commandment – Love your neighbour as yourself – and its corollary, Love your enemy too. Yet do we? The enemy as far as the majority of North American Christians is concerned is Communism, and yet we not only will not love the Communists, but we won't even talk with the people of China. I am not a fundamentalist, but when I see the blind lack of faith on this American Christian continent, which makes us put six hundred million Chinese in an ideological leper colony, I think Armageddon may well be soon upon us.

And my neighbour? In Canada we make it easier not to have a yellow or black neighbour. It does not become a problem because our immigration is strictly controlled. Has each one of us in the Church spoken out and acted against such discrimination? Or against discrimination closer to home? In Canada the Jew and the Negro are not welcomed as members in many clubs and neighbourhoods, and the general practices of discrimination against Indians and Eskimos are appalling.

If, then, the Church, which is ourselves, is really concerned with renewal, it must not only translate its services and its scriptures

ito language we can all understand. Each of its members must
ake personal responsibility for communicating with the world by
he quality of our lives. It must be supremely ironic for a man like
Martin Luther King to hear the rest of the Church talk about the
risis in communications. He has no difficulty getting his story
across in any media, because it is explosive, radical, and, above all,
Christian. When every person in a Christian Church on Sunday
tarts living a new life from Monday onwards – living *the* new life
i Jesus Christ – then the Church as a whole will have no trouble
etting its story across either.

## AN INTERVIEW WITH HARVEY COX

. Why, as a Christian, have you suggested that the word God be
ropped from our language for a time?
. I do not belong to the group of young theologians who feel that
ve have to work out some kind of a theology without God and
hat God is a meaningless entity. I think the problem is not so
nuch the reality or the experience as it is the word. The word God
as become so ambiguous; it means so many different things to so
nany different people, that it is almost impossible to use the word
i any useful way. I say the word, and something comes into your
nind; something else comes into another person's mind. It has
ecome a kind of catch-all phrase for anything anyone wants to
ut into it. For some people it is almost a nickname for supersti-
ion. For others, it has a connotation very close to what the Bible
neant by God. So I suggest that we ought to be a lot more re-
trained. We ought to talk less about God. In the Old Testament,
he Israelites never used the word for God. Once a year, the High
riest went into the Holy of Holies and by himself, spoke His
ame. In the New Testament too, there are those passages where
esus commends not everyone who says 'Lord, Lord,' but "those
vho do the work of my Father." So I think we ought to talk a lot

less, to put more emphasis on the life of the church, the sacrificial participation of Christian people in the world, and then see what language develops out of our engagement with the world.

We've also used God far too much as a concept to patch up the holes in our own thinking – as a kind of question answerer rather than as a question mark. For hundreds of years, what we couldn't explain, we attributed to God. But as science advanced and answered the questions that we couldn't answer without bringing God in, it has given God a smaller space. We can no longer accept this use of God as a kind of excuse for our own ignorance. The Bible is more concerned with the God who is the judge or the question mark or the interrogator. The Book of Job is particularly significant for us today. When Job runs into all his problems, when his whole theology is shot, when his family is taken by the plague and his house destroyed, God finally speaks to him. But He doesn't tell him anything. He asks a question, "Who is this that darkeneth my counsel without wisdom?" And he puts twenty or twenty-five questions to Job. This is the style of theology that we've got to move back to. God is the one who questions rather than the one who supplies little answers where our answers fail.

One reason why it's important to be a Christian in this secular world is that God also puts questions to the secularists. The secular person also needs to be questioned, because his secular point of view can become a closed system, an idol or an object of worship, unless it is constantly criticized and seen from a perspective which might demand that he change or open up new possibilities. The Church and the Christian live in society more to raise questions where questions are not being asked, than they do to provide answers, especially where these tend to be answers to questions which people are no longer asking.

Q. The main theme of your book is secularization. What exactly is this and how does it differ from secularism?

A. Secularization is a process within history, a process of opening up history, of delivering people from a closed understanding of what the world is and of what human life is. It is a process of delivering people from mythologies or from closed metaphysical systems, and of giving the responsibility for life, for the world, for society, to men themselves. Now I think that the process is not simply an accident. It started largely because of the impact of the Biblical faith on the world. And it really represents a working out in Western society (and now in the whole world) of the values and insights of the Bible.

Secularism is a quite different thing. It is making a Godless view of the world into a new religion, into a new Orthodoxy in which there are no more ultimate questions to be asked. I'm against all "isms," since they try to provide a total and inclusive view of the world and of man. This is the kind of thing which Christians, above all, ought to be critical of.

Q. Would you say then, that the establishment of Christendom in the middle ages and the maintenance of its relics today, such as Spain or any other place which claims to be a Christian country, is an aberration from the Biblical tradition?

A. Yes I would, and I think the period of the Kingship in Israel represented the same kind of thing that Christendom represents in Western civilization. The attempt to include all of a society's life and culture within a kind of sacral civilization is not true to the basic impulse of the biblical faith.

Q. What do you say to the churchgoer who, in our country at least, writes letters to the editor and says, since this is a Christian country, the state-supported schools should teach the Christian religion?

A. Christians should be concerned that the country they live in is one which allows them to practise their faith and allows those of other faiths to practise theirs. To achieve this there has to be an openness on the social level – just as on the philosophical level. Whenever there is only one alternative, one possibility of life presented and people are therefore not required to make choices, then I think we have lost ground. One contribution of the biblical faith to western culture has been to provide choices for man, to provide options for the way society can live.

Q. What do you mean by a theology of revolution?

A. There are enormous concentrations of wealth and privilege in one section of the world, and enormous underprivilege, anger, resentment, and hatred in another section. I think it is futile to believe that we in North America are simply going to chug along

comfortably the way we have been for the next decade withou
some very radical changes in our world. I think the people livin
in the underdeveloped areas are going to engage in revolution
And that unless we as Christians understand revolution as a way
in which God acts in history to bring justice and healing, salvatior
and restoration to man, we are lost.

The difficulty is that we have inherited a way of responding to
the world in which we see ourselves as a stabilizing influence, as
guardian of the values of the past, when in fact we may now be
required to discern and proclaim how God is at work in the worlc
turning things over, changing things, making things new, castin
down the mighty from their seats as the Gospel of Matthew put
it. To see this requires a theological awareness and appreciatior
of revolution. Not necessarily an automatic approval but ar
appreciation of revolution which will enable the Christians whc
live in underdeveloped countries to be a part of their revolution
and to enable North Americans to respond to revolution more
imaginatively.

Most modern revolutions – liberal, communist, American Negrc
– have derived ultimately from the biblical belief that all men are
brothers and have a common assignment from God to be the
sharers and custodians and co-creators of this world. But revolutions can become narrow in a racist or nationalist way. All the
more reason, then, for Christians to be active and present in them
participating when they can, criticizing when they must.

# SEVEN

## DIALOGUE WITH MYSELF

DIALOGUE WITH MYSELF

*by Pierre Berton*

Pierre Berton, the well-known Canadian writer and television personality is the author of twelve books including The Comfortable Pew and the award-winning Klondike, The Mysterious North, and Just Add Water and Stir. A former managing editor of Maclean's and associate editor and columnist of the Toronto Daily Star, he is now editor-in-chief of The Canadian Centennial Library. Apart from his books, he has written innumerable articles, radio, television, and film scripts, and revue sketches and songs. A regular panellist on the Canadian Broadcasting Corporation's "Front Page Challenge," he has had his own national television show since 1960.

**Pierre Berton**

## DIALOGUE WITH MYSELF

SELF: Well, the tumult and the shouting have died and the name-calling is almost at an end. The adjectives have all been used up: shallow, superficial, profound, prophetic, hasty, ill-advised, accurate, pretentious, insufferable, powerful, incisive, pompous, ignorant, atheistic, Christian. So what do you think about it all?

ME: You know, I find myself agreeing with almost everything that's been said, even when it's contradictory; because, you see, I think a pretty good case can be made *against The Comfortable Pew*, just as I think a pretty good case can be made for it. When I read some of the pieces in this book I was nagged by the usual self-doubts which assail any author who suffers from the fear that he may have been too glib. I could make an excellent case against my own book.

SELF: What would you say?

ME: I'd say, in a nutshell, that it bore the signs of being hastily-written, that it left out vast areas of Christian concern, that it wasn't nearly trenchant enough in certain areas, and that in places it was superficial, contradictory, and confused. How's that for a start?

SELF: So you agree that it could have been a better book. If you'd given it more time, study, and thought you might have produced a lasting work of real literary quality.

ME: Perhaps. But then I didn't set out to write a "good" book. I set out to write an *effective* book and that's a different thing. *The Comfortable Pew* comes closer to propaganda than it does to literature and this was the intention of sponsor and author alike. I'll tell you a secret: at one time I thought of asking the Church people to give me another year; but I decided against it. The book was designed as an instrument for action. If it has been effective, much of its value lies in its timing. If I *had* taken another year and produced a "better" book, I do not believe it would have been as useful. It seemed to me then that the book had to be published as soon as possible, and I think the results have borne me out. It may be that its content wasn't as important as the *event* of its publication.

SELF: The critics are right, you know: the book is full of generalities and oversimplifications, and there are great areas of legitimate criticism that you've ignored.

ME: The same thing can be said of most sermons, including the good ones. There's nothing wrong with generalities providing you label them as such. The book *could* have been hedged with qualifications; it *could* have been three times as long; it *could* have been more profound – more "literary," if you like. But under those conditions I think it would have been much harder going for the people I wanted to reach. It was designed to pack a wallop.

SELF: So! You admit you set out deliberately to be as controversial as possible. Doesn't it make you cringe to be called a professional controversialist?

ME: It makes me cringe only because I admit nothing of the sort. I was asked to launch what the church calls "a dialogue" and to take a position in that dialogue. I did what any good debater does when he wants to provoke rebuttal. But if the dialogue has been effectively launched, it is because the views I expressed were honestly held.

SELF: Oh, *come* now! Surely you expected a controversy and surely you revelled in it.

ME: I expected to be attacked, but none of us really expected a controversy of the proportions this one achieved. I revel in the fact that the book was more effective than I thought it would be. I thought most of what I said was self-evident, and I was astonished that things which seemed self-evident to me should have provoked such a reaction.

SELF: But that's what many of your critics said – that there was nothing new in the book, nothing fresh: just "a pretty collection of anti-Christian clichés that have been kicking around high school and university student cafés for half a century or more."

ME: Well, *that* irritates me. In my original preface I wrote: "I would not pretend that there is much in this book that is new. Most of what I have to say has been said before in various ways, and often more eloquently, by others. Many of these have been practising Christians and clergymen. . . ." A raft of critics act as if they had made this discovery independently.

Of course the ideas in the book weren't new. I've held many of them for more than twenty years. After all, that's why I left the Church. Still, you know, an opinion doesn't have to be new to be valid or effective. The Church holds some that are two thousand years old.

New or old, a great deal of what I said has either angered or stimulated or goaded some tens of thousands of readers and clerics, perhaps because it was, in one reviewer's phrase, "the expression of thoughts the reader has had in the back of his mind for some time but has never expressed." It's interesting, but not surprising, that some of the most favourable reviews of the book have come from the clergy and some of the angriest from critics who are atheists, agnostics, or nothings. To these latter critics much of the book is, indeed, old stuff and they rightly ask from their point of view: "What's all the fuss about? We've been saying this for years." But the book was not written for atheists; it was written for Anglican churchgoers. The letters I've received from these people suggest that, though the ideas in the book aren't really very new, they are new to these people in the sense that they haven't been exposed to them in straightforward print before. I saw it as part of my task to express in simple terms certain critiques of organized religion that had heretofore been expressed more obscurely, if more profoundly. So, when a lady in Saskatchewan writes to say she needed to look up only one word in the dictionary I take it as high praise.

SELF: So then you're not much more than a popularizer – a kind of ecclesiastical rewrite man?

ME: Perhaps more. A synthesizer, too, and maybe a catalyst. And you know there *are* one or two things in the book that might be described as fairly new – much *too* new for some people. I hesitate to bring up the matter of sex and the Church's attitude to it again, because to do so is to rub a fingernail against the blackboard of conventional morality, but that passage is only a couple of years old. When the critics say there's nothing new in the book, they sometimes mean that the parts they agree with are "old stuff"; they ignore the rest.

SELF: All the same, you've got to admit the truth of such remarks as Ruth Taylor's in *The Churchman* that many of the criticisms you make "aren't so true today as they were ten years ago," and that you really didn't take into account the enormous revolution that's been going on inside the Church.

ME: I suppose I should have paid more attention to it. Certainly I was exposed to it. After all the commissioning of the book was part of that revolution. But the Church has yet to live down its past. And, to be brutally frank about it, I'm not convinced that the revolution is nearly as extensive as the insiders seem to believe it is. Part of this, perhaps, has to do with the Church's inability to communicate with the world. When I started on the book I had only the vaguest idea of the ferment within the Anglican community. The event of the book's publication has helped to change that – and there's a paradox. The public has now been *told*, in this way, that something has happened. I wonder if it has also been *shown*.

SELF: Oh, come off it! How about the thousands of clergymen who were involved last year in demonstrations, such as Selma? How about the Viet Nam protests, the switch of position by the Anglicans on divorce, the change in the Sunday School curriculum? The examples are legion. Surely there *is* a fresh breeze blowing through the Church, and surely the evidence of that clean wind is everywhere.

ME: Yes, but I'm not at all certain that this constitutes revolution. It seems to me that a lot of it is just the Church catching up on issues that were once too hot to handle and are now safely respectable. The Church sometimes confuses this catching-up-with-the-past with progress.

In *The Comfortable Pew* I made reference to nineteenth century missionary practice which several of my church critics have, I think, purposely chosen to misread in their zeal to prove things have changed. They keep saying that I am away behind the times because missionary work in Africa and Asia has undergone a revolution. I'm well aware of that and tried to make it clear in my book. For I was using the old missionary image to make a point about the Church's role in Canada. I wrote that "the same kind of refusal to adapt to native conditions operates in the latter half of the twentieth century in Western society." By native conditions I meant, of course, conditions in Canadian suburban parishes, not Congo villages.

The question is this: A generation from now will another writer in another critical book be able to say that the Church in the 1960's continued to cater to the comfortable pew by ignoring the uncomfortable issues that lay just below the surface? After all, most of the causes I outlined already belong to the past. Mopping-up operations may continue but the real battles have been won. Birth control may seem a lively controversy today, but in the Protestant world at least it is no longer an uncomfortable one. Back in 1912 it was uncomfortable, just as the racial issue was uncomfortable in the twenties and thirties and the nuclear issue uncomfortable in the forties and early fifties. The Church must continue to take a position on these matters but it must also try to understand and come to grips with the problems of present and future. Some of these problems, and the Church's general inattention to them, have been outlined by William Stringfellow in his excellent essay in this book.

SELF: But isn't it the most difficult thing in the world to sense what the real problems are, as opposed to the pretend problems?

ME: Agreed. Certainly we are groping in at least two areas: the sexual area and the area of work and leisure; not that we all necessarily hold old-fashioned attitudes in these areas but simply that we don't know how to cope with new social patterns.

But there's one uncomfortable issue that is fairly obvious. That is what I would call the New Racial Problem as opposed to the Old Racial Problem. The Old Racial Problem had to do with the unequal treatment of minority racial groups within the bounds of our own country – with job opportunities, housing, public attitudes, and so on. The New Racial Problem has to do with the same inequalities on a world scale: the presence of overly-rich white nations living within a jet-plane ride of underdeveloped coloured nations. These white nations, two of which inhabit the mansion of North America, give alms to the poor; but they are not so Christian that they will let the poor into the mansion.

I made some passing reference to this in a passage in *The Comfortable Pew*, which several critics have chosen to misread. I compared the poor of our time – the masses of India, Asia, and Africa – to the poor of an earlier period pressing their faces against the windows of the chateau. The chateau is now a continent, and the window is symbolic; but the faces continue to press against it pleading for admittance. I was astonished to discover several

critics taking my imagery literally and upbraiding me for failing
to realize that the Church has always helped the poor. I think one
man even used the Fred Victor Mission in Toronto as an example!
SELF: But are these political matters properly the concern of the
Church? Can the Church really take a unified stand as an institution on this sort of thing? One of the criticisms of your book, and
a fairly widely-held one, was that this sort of matter is really
outside the Church's province: that there are many varying stands
a Christian can take –

ME: I want to go into that in detail later. But really, you know, a
very large section of the Christian Church *has* now made up its
mind on the subject of racial brotherhood; otherwise we wouldn't
have had so many ministers in the Selma parades. Some issues are
complex and difficult, but as Rabbi Fackenheim points out in his
perceptive piece in this volume, "With racial justice, the required
stand is straightforward." And what we are talking about is racial
injustice as we see it selfishly reflected in the immigration policies
we tacitly support.

Recently I attended a discussion on *The Comfortable Pew* at an
Anglican church, and we got onto this subject. I suggested that
the Church either meant what it said or else it was being hypocritical. Unless my hearing is faulty, the scriptures tell us in a
variety of ways that we are our brother's keeper. I suggested,
therefore, that if the Church wanted to demonstrate that it meant
on Monday what it said from the altar and pulpit on Sunday, it
had no other course than to press for wide-open immigration
policy, regardless of race, creed, colour, or training. This remark
produced some interesting reactions. A leading layman stood up
and said bluntly that such a policy was impractical. It would
cause us all (we whites) to lose jobs. It would force us to adopt
a lower standard of living. The country would be flooded with
unskilled workers, and we'd have to spend money training them.
We'd suffer from unheard-of racial problems. Again it may be
that my perception is faulty, and that, as some critics insist, I do
not understand what the Church's leaders have been saying over
the years and that I misread the implications of the gospels; yet
I must persist in my belief that everything this layman was saying, while undeniably true, was also undeniably un-Christian. A
cry for a wide-open immigration policy is perhaps impractical but

when did practicality ever enter into the basic teachings of the Christian Church? "Take all thou hast and give to the poor" appears to some to be manifestly impractical. "Consider the lilies of the field; they toil not, neither do they spin" is at odds with the practicality of a work-oriented society. "Turn the other cheek" is scarcely practical in a war economy. "Thou shalt not covet" hardly fits the practical necessities of modern advertising. The Church has for years been preaching the virtues of impracticality without ever being prepared to accept the sacrifices of its consequences. This is why so many people see it as a hypocritical institution. I say the time has come for the Church to put up or shut up. Let it show that it believes what it says, and what its Messiah said, or let it rewrite the Scriptures.

The reaction of the minister of that particular church was as interesting as that of his laymen. He announced that he would be prepared to set up a committee to look into the matter. I really believe he thought he was on my side of the dialogue. But what he was really doing, with the best of intentions, was squirming out of an uncomfortable situation. Is a committee needed to dig out the unappetising facts? They are simple and widely understood: We live in the richest and emptiest continent in the world. Just across the water from this roomy continental palace, black and yellow people exist in grinding poverty, crowded together amid filth, disease, despair, and death. What is the Christian attitude to these people? To keep them in the ghetto and send them tracts, missionaries, and the occasional crust? Or to let them into the mansion? Yet anyone who advocates such a policy will be attacked first as naive and impractical and later as dangerous and demented – adjectives, I suppose, that were in use some two thousand years ago in Jerusalem. He will encounter the bitterest and most violent opposition from organized capital and organized labour. It will be pointed out that such a policy will not work, since it would quickly cause hardship, hunger, unemployment, loss of income, and property rights – meaning, of course, that it would cause these ills among white Christian Canadians. All this is no doubt true. Our standard of living would certainly drop. But what has one's standard of living got to do with Christianity? The causes of an unfettered, or even of a limited, immigration policy from the underdeveloped countries are awesome to contemplate: for the first time millions of people who pay lip service to the Christian ideals of the brotherhood of man and universal voluntary love would actually be forced to do some of the same things their Christ did; to move on the same level as the halt, the sick, the afflicted, the lonely, the hungry, and the cast-offs of this world – and not as observers, but as part of the motley, anguished throng.

SELF: I suspect you've got your tongue in your cheek. You don't really believe in a policy of unlimited immigration any more than you believe in a policy of total disarmament. You know very well that it's impractical and foolish.

ME: Yes, I probably do. But when I tell my friends in the clergy that much of Christianity seems to me impossible to attain, and for many of the same reasons, they tell me that Christianity is itself an ideal and that, even though we can't achieve it perfectly, we ought to strive for it. If this is so, then again I say the Church's anointed ought to be advocating the impossible, impractical, but very Christian idea of unlimited immigration.

SELF: And you? It's all very well to say these things from your own comfortable pew. Would you personally be willing to accept the consequences of the action you say the Church should press for? Are you prepared to divide your acreage into small parcels to accommodate the overpopulation that would result? Are you prepared to see your income dwindle to the point where you and your family might go hungry? In a pig's eye you are!

ME: I don't view it with any particular relish. It would all be very uncomfortable and distressing – almost as distressing as living in Calcutta as an untouchable. If you ask me if I intend today to parcel up my land, home, and income, I'd say no. I'm not strong enough to do it by myself, I guess. But if all of us – neighbours, friends, strangers, chance acquaintances – were in the same boat, as one is in wartime, say, it might be possible to bear. It might even be exciting, as war often is, and not really as dangerous in the end if you want to be practical; since it might remove the chief cause of war and thus, uncomfortable or not, be somewhat preferable to the inevitable alternative of out-and-out destruction. But these are not really Christian considerations. My real point is that, in my own naiveté, I cannot, after reading the

Gospels and listening to my clerical friends, see any other stand for the Church to take.

SELF: Oh you can't, can't you? Isn't that one of the most telling criticisms of your book? That you, of all people, who criticize the Church in the sexual area, for instance, because it insists on a code of absolutes – you, yourself, are laying down rules of absolute conduct for the Church and these absolutes very often tend to be little more than a reflection of your own small "I" liberal views. Aren't you, too, suffering "pretensions to absolute rightness"?

ME: I suppose I am. The dilemma which I suffer from is the same as the one that afflicts the Church. The only difference is that we are on opposite sides of the same coin. What I was trying to say was this: If the Church insists on taking absolute positions in such fields as that of sexual morality then it must be prepared to be criticized for not taking absolute positions in such fields as business ethics, war, racial injustice, and so on. It can't have things both ways.

SELF: But that doesn't let you off the hook, does it? You advocate a flexible position in the area of sexual morality – something like the views of some British Quakers[1] – but an absolute position on, for instance, warfare. Surely that's inconsistent.

ME: I said we were on two sides of the same coin. But what I did not make clear in the book is that there is a considerable difference between what I personally think, and what I believe the Church has to do if it is to act in accordance with its own words. I am not, for instance, an out-and-out pacifist, in the sense that some Christians are pacifist. I would not advocate unilateral disarmament. I would not have opposed and did not oppose World War II. There are conditions, I think, under which I might still advocate armed revolution though such things are much more difficult to advocate in a nuclear age. But then I do not call myself a Christian. The churchmen around me, however, continue to talk of peace . . . peace . . . peace. The word is dragged out at Christmastime and made synonymous with Christianity. Yet some of the very men who talk so glibly of the Prince of Peace are to be found symbolically or literally blessing weapons and passively accepting in the name of wartime expediency every kind of human villainy from the indiscriminate bombing of civilians to the torture of Viet Cong prisoners.

It is not that I have attacked the Church because it sometimes fails to share my personal social and political convictions. It is because it appears to be failing to follow its *own* convictions. The Church of England, as I pointed out, *has* come to a conclusion about the use of nuclear weapons. But it took fourteen years for it to make up its mind. Surely what turned out to be an offense against God in 1964 was also an offense against God at the time of Hiroshima.

One area of social concern, which I did not deal with, may serve to make my point. Though some of the clergy still argue that hanging is necessary to the safety of a civilized society, I doubt that any now believe, as many once believed, that seven-year-olds should be strung up for pilfering spoons or traitors publicly disembowelled. In that sense, the whole body of the Christian Church has come to a definite and absolute conclusion. But it ought to be remembered that the English bishops were among the last to change their minds on these points.

SELF: But really now, can any large Protestant denomination with its emphasis on individual conscience and its absence of totalitarian authority – can it ever take a consistently strong position on such issues?

ME: Perhaps not, though, as I have pointed out, it eventually does. But it can change the climate to allow, nay, even encourage more radicals in its midst and to allow these radicals more expression.

SELF: But don't you think it does that? Look, for instance, at Bishop Pike in the States or Bishop Robinson in Britain. Look at the Red Dean. Look at some of the men who commissioned *The Comfortable Pew*.

ME: Right! But such men still seem to me to be in the minority.

SELF: Won't they always be? Haven't they always been?

ME: If the church is to survive and grow, their number will have to increase.

SELF: But what's stopping that increase? Surely not the hierarchy of the Church?

ME: To some extent the hierarchy. To some extent the system – the institutionalism which flourishes only when the status quo is maintained. To some extent the large mass of the laity who continue to prefer their pews comfortable.

SELF: *So!* you blame the laymen, do you? You virtually ignored the large mass of the laity in your book. You airily defined "the Church" as the hierarchy and leadership when the real Church is the whole body of Christ – worshippers and priests combined. They ticked you off for that, didn't they?

ME: Oh, yes; though why a man should be blamed for explicitly defining his terms of reference at the outset, I don't know.

SELF: Surely those terms of reference were too narrow.

ME: If they were any wider I should not have been writing a critique of the Church but a critique of Canadian society. By "leadership," of course, I meant to include leading laymen – but certainly not the followers to whose comfort, I still insist, the leadership often caters. I cannot agree that my definition of the Church was too far away from what both clergy and laymen mean when they commonly use that phrase – or from what some of the writers in this book mean when they use it. After all, when somebody criticizes General Motors, they mean the management and board of directors; they certainly aren't including all the widows who happen to own a few shares of voting stock. I suggest that analogy isn't too far out.

SELF: But in a sense weren't you attacking Canadian society in spite of your narrower terms of reference? One critic said that you set up "a woozy straw man – the Church" and that you then used that term as an omnibus clause into which you lumped all that you found wrong with modern society.

ME: Well, perhaps. That's probably the sort of thing I myself would write if I were given the job of reviewing *The Comfortable Pew*. But then, one of the points I made was that the institution of the Church is sometimes indistinguishable from the institution of society as a whole.

SELF: Is that necessarily bad?

ME: If you believe that a kinetic social institution should be more than a mere reflection of the world around it, then it's bad. Remember, I was asked to point out what I personally thought was wrong with the Church. I said that I thought the Church would have to lead, not follow, if it was to survive and be respected. Thus it has to be in tension with society. I say it isn't.

SELF: But haven't you made the very serious error of equating Christianity with liberalism? Rabbi Fackenheim makes this point pretty tellingly in this book.

ME: I don't mean to suggest that Christianity and liberalism are the same thing, but I do think that liberalism – certainly my kind – is a reflection of the Christian concern for the individual. I suppose we can argue forever about the liberal tradition and where it springs from, but I would say that part of it springs out of the Christian tradition. It occurs to me that it is very difficult for the churchman to follow certain of the precepts of Christ and not find himself, from time to time, sharing the same highway with the liberal. Liberalism and Christianity often do meet on common ground, and it is on this ground, in my opinion, that the Church has sometimes been found wanting.

SELF: But once again I think you can't slither off the hook as easily as all that. You've got to admit that William Stringfellow has got you neatly trapped when he says that you admit your conviction that God *does* prefer Western democracy to all others. How do you equate that with your earlier message about God not being on *anyone's* side?

ME: I can't; and on the evidence of my own words, he's got me. I've read that passage again and I'm appalled by it. All I can say – and it sounds pretty weak – is that I didn't mean it the way it sounds. I said, correctly, I think, that Christian concepts are part of our heritage, that they form the basis of many Western attitudes, and that our national conscience, springing from this heritage, can when aroused shape the course of history for the betterment of mankind. I didn't mean to suggest that Western democracy has an exclusive lien on Christian concepts, and I hope the rest of the book makes that clear. I think the United Church was correct to call Communism a Christian heresy and it is possible that (distressing as this will sound to some) this Christian heresy may have more to do with bettering mankind than our Christian Western society. I would further agree with Mr. Stringfellow that from the Christian point of view all idolatry of nation and worship of national ideology ought to be protested and exposed.

SELF: Which brings us, in a roundabout way, to the question that has really been eating at you. Is Christianity an instrument of political action or of personal reconciliation? What have the Gospels to do, really, with any system of morals or ethics? And don't you, as Stringfellow charges, fail to distinguish between radical ethical idealism and voluntary love?

ME: If I fail to make that distinction so does the Church. Stringfellow writes that the Churches are content "merely to echo the secular ethics of humanism." I would agree and to me the damaging word is "echo." If the Church is merely the echo of a secular society, then there is no real reason for the Church to exist at all. I think I have had something to say about Christian love in my book, and if, on occasion, I have equated the requirements of human love with the demands of a radical ethical system, I make no apology for it.

Furthermore, there is no reason why churchmen, in preaching about voluntary love, grace, sacramental action, and personal reconciliation (Stringfellow's words) cannot make use of some sound examples rooted in the contemporary situation, to underline their message. Indeed, in those contemporary areas where love is denied, where the Devil is dominant, where Christ is blasphemed, and where the Gospel is profaned, then surely it is the duty of the Church to speak out – not on humanist terms, necessarily, but on its own.

Let me take one aspect of the conflict in South Viet Nam as an example. There is an honest argument, I suppose, on which Christians may differ regarding the practical as well as the moral pros and cons of that war. But can any Christian or any humanist condone for an instant the torture of enemy prisoners as a means of getting information about the other side? The newspapers tend to cover these horror tales in much the same way that they cover a fracas in the Maple Leaf Gardens, "objectively" with impersonal stories and deadpan captions. We are shown one prisoner with a knife placed against his belly; another with his head submerged in a tub of water; a third being flailed with clubs. We are told of terrified prisoners forced to watch one of their number tossed from a helicopter in flight as an object lesson in the dangers of not "co-operating," i.e. not betraying one's comrades. The ultimate horror of all this is the callous ease with which these matters have been accepted by the vast majority of newspaper readers and, it seems, newspaper writers, most of them at least nominally Christian. One might have expected a massive, continental wail of anguish. Instead, though there have been some notable individual protests, there has been much more official and unofficial justification, some of it implied, some of it direct.

As far as I can determine, the justification for this monstrous offense against humanity in South Viet Nam (and, surely, from the Church's point of view against Christ) can be summed up as follows:

1 "Everybody's doing it." The other side is far worse than we are. It's a rough war after all and we've got to fight fire with fire – use the enemy's own tactics if we want to win.

2 We're *forced* to do it. It's the only way we can win. Sure, it's horrible but it's better that a few individuals suffer pain than that thousands die – especially American boys.

3 It's not really our doing. White westerners don't actually engage in torture. It's the Vietnamese that do these awful things. Our people are only observers. It's an internal matter in which we can't interfere.

4 After all, they're only Asians and they're used to it. Physical torture is almost a way of life with them.

Perhaps I misread my scriptures, but it seems to me that all of this is blasphemous. The Christian may attack it on different grounds than the humanist but attack it he must. If I'm wrong; if I *do* misread my scriptures; if this sort of horror is *not* a matter of insistent Christian concern; if it is generally held that the Church should not cry out in protest when human beings are mangled in the name of expediency; then all I can say is that I lose all vestige of interest in the Church and in Christianity; it is not for me; if it fades and dies tomorrow, I shall not mourn.

SELF: But there you go again, talking in terms of principles and not in terms of individuals. You know very well that churchmen have always protested this kind of thing and will continue to do so; but you also know that the Church has another role, which you have largely ignored. That is to reach out to the suffering – not just the physical sufferers in a remote corner of the globe at a specific moment in history but those who come heavy-laden and in anguish to its doors at all times and in all places, tortured not by knives and clubs but by an inner ferment compounded of loneliness or self-hate or fear or guilt or any of those other ills of the spirit of which Elizabeth Kilbourn writes so movingly in the prologue to this book. It is to these people that ministers minister – yes and sometimes, as you sneeringly put it, while balancing teacups on their knees – and this kind of traditional ministration and the need for it is glossed over in your book.

ME: I have no real answer to that charge except to say that *The Comfortable Pew* is a personal book and in no sense definitive. I was asked to write what I personally found wrong with the Church, not what I found right with it. I supposed when I wrote the book I felt that in this area of individual ministry the Church was less open to criticism than in some of the other areas I outlined.

SELF: Did you, really? Or did you simply feel that it didn't matter?

ME: Perhaps I did. Certainly by ignoring it I indicated that I did. But if I thought it unimportant, I erred, for I no longer think so.

SELF: But why did you think it unimportant? Why did you dismiss it? Come on – face me.

ME: I suspect it was because I knew, deep within myself, that if I were suffering from the kind of personal anguish which Mrs. Kilbourn describes I would not turn to the Church for solace.

SELF: And why not?

ME: Because for me, and I think for many thousands of others like me, the Church by its failure in those other fields which matter to me, has rendered itself impotent to help me as an individual. I simply cannot respect it.

SELF: But surely you are confused here. Surely a sufferer does not seek solace from some*thing* but from some*one*. Your critics have pointed out that you sometimes seem to ignore the fact that the Church is composed of individuals. And surely it is an individual clergyman or priest whom they have come to respect that the poor, the bruised, and the blind seek out when their burdens become intolerable. You may be disillusioned with the institutional garment of the Church; you may be embarrassed and sickened by its postures; but can you say that, within the framework of that amazing institution, there are not individuals whom you respect and to whom you might easily turn, if, as many some day happen, you can no longer cope with the cares and complexities of this world?

ME: It's quite possible. It's equally possible that I might turn to a friend or acquaintance whom I admire and who is outside the Church.

SELF: The Church would say, in that case, that Christ was working in that person and thus you *were* turning to Christ.

ME: No doubt; and perhaps the Church would be right, though I often think it uses that device to get itself off the hook. It doesn't alter my original point: that whenever the Church bankrupts itself in one area of concern, it tends to bankrupt itself in others. By its own failure to come to grips with this world it loses its power to make *me* come to grips with the next.

SELF: Aha! You talk of the "next world," do you? And you call yourself an agnostic!

ME: I use it symbolically to mean the world that is not Caesar's. For want of a better phrase I don't mind calling it the "spiritual world." It exists within each of us. Whether or not it continues after we die, I don't know. I would doubt it.

SELF: It's strange to hear you using that word "spiritual." You certainly kept away from spiritual matters in your book. You rarely mentioned the Bible.

ME: If the Church had wanted a theological critique it would undoubtedly have commissioned a theologian to write *The Comfortable Pew*. As for the Bible: no, I didn't quote extensively from it. I assumed my readers had read it. Certainly a knowledge of the New Testament is by implication requisite to an understanding of the book.

SELF: You obviously agree with a good deal that's in the New Testament, especially the Sermon on the Mount. Many churchmen have said that your book shows a real concern for the survival of Christian faith. If so, then why don't you get in there and pitch? Why don't you join the Church? It's all very well to throw stones from the sidelines; but wouldn't you be more effective working from within?

ME: When I was writing a daily column, often critical of various social institutions to which I did not specifically belong, I was continually faced with this question. I suppose every social critic meets the same challenge. Perhaps by our very natures we are not joiners; certainly we cannot join everything. I *am* concerned about the survival of the Christian faith but not necessarily of the Christian Church.

SELF: But if the faith is to live, surely the Church in some form must continue.

ME: I hope not in its present form. Let me make a not-entirely-frivolous parallel. I happen to agree with and applaud several of the service aims of the Kiwanis Club. I think the Kiwanians do a great deal of good in this world, and I would like to see this attitude of service prevail. But to me, the idea of attending a Kiwanis luncheon every week is so appalling that I would move to Zanzibar before I would become an active member.

SELF: Are you really telling me that you equate the Christian Church with a mere service club?

ME: In a sense, I suppose, I do. And maybe that's the most searing indictment I can make of the Church. What I'm saying is this: I consider the Church an important institution in society but it's not, for me, the *only* institution. The really important institution is society itself. Of that I am a member and I hope a reasonably active one.

SELF: But there's more to it than that, now isn't there?

ME: Yes. There's more to it. The other reason I don't belong is simply that the Church asks me to recite regularly a series of statements that I cannot take on faith. Specifically it asks me to believe, and to say aloud that I believe, in life after death, in the divinity of Christ, in the Resurrection of the body and in certain other matters. I think thousands like me face this dilemma and are troubled by it. I might like to believe in these things; I might be more comfortable holding such beliefs; but, in point of fact I do *not* believe such things and I'm damned if I'm going to say I do when I don't. Moreover, I don't even think it is necessary to believe in such things to be a decent human being, to live a good, worthwhile and rewarding life, and even to be a "Christian," though that is a matter of semantics.

SELF: But aren't you aware that there are many churchmen – and some very important ones – who don't take these things literally, either? If they work within the institutional framework of the Church, why can't you?

ME: Maybe they have a different temperament, I don't know.

Maybe they've stopped listening to what it is they say aloud every Sunday. Maybe they treat the prayers and hymns and even parts of the Gospels as we treat folksongs. Maybe they feel they're more effective as human beings inside the Church. That's their business. All I can say is I can't do it. And personally I think I've been more effective on the outside.

SELF: All of this sounds a bit odd in the light of the last few pages of your book in which you seem to predict and to welcome a Second Coming. . . .

ME: That, it turns out, is the most controversial section of *The Comfortable Pew* and I find *that* a bit odd. Several critics whom I admire have written that I am "beseeching" a new Christ to come down to earth or that I am "yearning" nostalgically for another Messiah or that I am "calling" for a Second Coming. I'm afraid, however, that these final pages are rooted in a deeper pessimism than seems apparent. I happen to be in agreement with Jim Lotz who wrote in the University of B.C.'s student paper that "it is not to the actions or to the promise of a single man that mankind must look. It is to themselves." If man is ultimately to be free of all dependencies, if he is to throw away his crutches, then that is certainly true. Alas, I see no prospect of such un-fettered liberty. When I wrote at the conclusion of *The Comfortable Pew* that revolution – *real* revolution within the Church – would most probably come (if, indeed, it comes at all) through the actions of a single man, a traditional Suffering Servant, I wasn't advocating anything or even yearning for anything, but simply outlining the most likely of several roads to change. I hold to this. The state of the Church being what it is, I still suspect that violent change is likelier to come as the result of the emer-gence of a single, passionate, selfless leader than by any spon-taneous mass action.

SELF: What you are really underlining is your lack of faith in the adulthood of man – something you insisted had arrived.

ME: No; in the adulthood of the Church – something I've insisted hasn't arrived.

SELF: Don't you think it's possible that the change may come not from a single leader and not from spontaneous mass action, as you put it, but from the emergence of a small but significant minority within the institution, each of whom may have, to some extent, those qualities which were Christ's and each of whom will make his witness and suffer his sacrifice?

ME: This is possible and even probable. There are signs that such a group is appearing now. How effective it can be is another matter. If it is effective, then I suspect that one man will stand out from this group. This has generally been the case. In the Negro revolution, which certainly has had its growing band of dedicated men and martyrs, one Messiah emerged, in the person of Martin Luther King, to electrify the movement into action. In India, there were many disciples, but only one Mahatma. I'm not sure this is necessarily a bad thing and I'm not sure that, if the Church is worth saving, it isn't inevitable.

SELF: How do you mean "if the Church is worth saving"?

ME: You and I have been wrestling over that question all along, haven't we? And, paradoxical though it may sound, I think we've come to a conclusion: If revolution doesn't come, then the Church isn't worth saving. But if the Church *is* worth saving, then revolution is as inevitable as it was in Mississippi or Bombay.

# NOTES

INTRODUCTION

[1] Harvey Cox, *The Secular City* (New York: The Macmillan Company, and London: S.C.M. Press, 1965).

RELIGION WITHOUT DOGMA

[1] John A. T. Robinson, *The New Reformation?* (London: S.C.M. Press, and Philadelphia: Westminster Press, 1965).

[2] Harvey Cox, *op. cit.*, Ch. VI.

[3] Colin W. Williams, *What in the World?* (New York: National Council of Christian Churches, 1964, and London: Epworth Press, 1965), p. 4.

FAITH WITH DOGMA

[1] Owen Chadwick, *The Reformation* (London: Penguin Books, 1964), p. 11.

[2] John A. T. Robinson, *op. cit.*, p. 19.

[3] James Pike, *A Time for Christian Candor* (New York: Harpers, 1964 and London: Hodder & Stoughton, 1965).

THE CATHOLIC TRADITION

[1] Donald M. Mathers, *A New Look at Belief* (Toronto: Ryerson Press, 1964), p. 1.

[2] Pierre Berton, *The Comfortable Pew* (Toronto: McClelland & Stewart Limited, and Philadelphia: J. B. Lippincott, Company, 1965).
[3] *Ibid.*, p. 140.

[4] *Ibid.*, pp. 126f.

[5] I Cor. 13:9.

6 I Cor. 13:12.

7 Thomas Aquinas, *Summa Theologiae*, Ia, q. 2, pref.

8 Pierre Berton, *op. cit.*, p. 127 and Thomas Aquinas, *Summa Theologiae*, IIa-IIae, q.1, a.2.

9 II Cor. 5:7.

10 Berton, *op. cit.*, p. 120.

11 *Ibid.*, p. 124.

12 *Ibid.*, p. 122.

13 *Ibid.*, p. 124.

14 II Cor. 5:19.

A JEW LOOKS AT CHRISTIANITY AND SECULARIST LIBERALISM

1 Roy Eckhardt, *The Journal of Bible and Religion*, vol. 33 No. 2 (April 1965), p. 124.

2 Frederick C. Grant, "Not All the Bishops Did Was Wise", *The Witness* XLIX, 35 (October 29, 1964), p. 9.

3 Eckhardt, *op. cit.*, p. 126.

DIALOGUE WITH MYSELF

1 Alastair Heron, ed., *Towards a Quaker View of Sex* (London: Friends' Home Service Committee), 1963.